Stories, Time and Again

Stories, Time and Again

A Program Guide for Schools and Libraries

Jan Irving

Illustrated by Joni Giarratano

LIBRARIES UNLIMITED

A Member of the Greenwood Publishing Group

Westport, Connecticut • London

Library of Congress Cataloging-in-Publication Data

Irving, Jan, 1942-
    Stories, time and again : a program guide for schools and libraries / Jan Irving ; illustrated by Joni Giarratano.
        p. cm.
    Includes bibliographical references and index.
    ISBN 1-56308-998-X (pbk. : alk. paper)
    1. Activity programs in education—United States. 2. Children's libraries—Activity programs—United States. 3. Children—Books and reading—United States. I. Giarratano, Joni, ill. II. Title.
LB1027.25.I78 2006
372.67'7—dc22   2005029419

British Library Cataloguing in Publication Data is available.

Library of Congress Catalog Card Number: 2005029419
ISBN: 1-56308-998-X

First published in 2006

Libraries Unlimited, 88 Post Road West, Westport, CT 06881
A Member of the Greenwood Publishing Group, Inc.
www.lu.com

Printed in the United States of America

The paper used in this book complies with the Permanent Paper Standard issued by the National Information Standards Organization (Z39.48–1984).

10   9   8   7   6   5   4   3   2   1

With love and respect time and again to my husband Bill,
my editor Barbara,
and all who share the power of stories.

Contents

Introduction

What do Albert Einstein, Robert Coles, and Scheherazade have in common? Although these three people pursued vastly different walks of life—a world famous scientist, an American physician and social activist, and the Persian storyteller of *The Thousand and One Nights*—all believed in the primary value of story. We all have our own testament to the value of story in our lives. Here are two of my favorites.

A little boy's mother read him the story of *The Clown of God.* The boy became fascinated with the tale of Giovanni who juggled fruits and vegetables. He began juggling produce in grocery stories much to his mother's dismay. Today as an adult, he juggles his job, family, and volunteer work. He also performs juggling workshops for children in his spare time.

A little girl worried that she wasn't like the other kids in her neighborhood. Then she read a book about a little girl who liked to pretend, to "skibble out of bed," and ride a hotel elevator "for Lord's sake." After she read *Eloise,* she knew it was OK to be different. No other person in her school grew up to be an author.

The premise behind my book *Stories NeverEnding* (Libraries Unlimited, 2004) attests to the importance of stories in our personal lives and in the world's cultures. This has always been the case. Since prehistory, stories have shaped civilizations and separated people from all other animals. Does this sound too remote from our postliterate world? Does story still have a place in an age when schools must concentrate on teaching basics so that students can pass standardized tests? Do public libraries have a purpose beyond providing computer games and Internet services? Stories, I firmly believe, are as important now as they have always been. They are the most powerful learning tools we have. In times of disaster, they seem even more vital because they draw us together. Stories of the people who died in the Twin Towers on September 11—stories that ran for months in the *New York Times*—comforted those of us who read them faithfully. We probably won't see a chain of stores named "Stories 'R Us," but I believe that this is true. One of my favorite books, *Teaching as Storytelling* by Kieran Egan, explains this more eloquently than I have.

The story form is a cultural universal; everyone everywhere enjoys stories. The story, then, is not just some casual entertainment; it reflects a basic and powerful form in which we make sense of the world and experience.

Stories, Time and Again continues the pattern of presenting school and library programs on ten topics with books and stories as the foundation. *Stories NeverEnding* covered the following topics: reading incentive programs, art and literature, food and literature, math and literature, humor, poetry, storytelling, booktalking, U.S. history, and courage and healing. This companion volume includes other topics found in the school curriculum and of interest to elementary school–age children. Those topics are as follows: the Middle Ages, tropical rainforests, Australian animals, Egyptian mythology, folk literature, creative dramatics, manners and bullying, friends, biographies, and fantasy. Some subjects in this newer volume overlap with topics in the first volume, such as those on storytelling and creative dramatics. The topics of friends and manners correlate to the subject of power through books on courage and healing. Even the chapter on folk literature focuses on using brains and bravery instead of brawn to succeed.

Both books emphasize language skills in content areas. Although I have not used the terminology or "rubrics" of "Six Trait Writing" familiar to most elementary teachers, the principles of clear organization, good word choice, solid content, establishing a personal voice, and writing fluently are taught through the many writing activities in this book. Script writing, creating original fantasies, and retelling folktales appear in many chapters. New ideas for writing reports and "book blurbs" will help students focus on nonfiction writing. Even more opportunities for oral expression are developed. In addition to creative dramatics, reader's theatre, and storytelling, in many chapters, the teacher and librarian will find suggestions for unusual oral reports, interviewing, and engaging in role-play activities to solve problems.

I have created original models in this book for doing research, creating scripts, making "skit kits," and introducing drama in different content areas through a "Drama Pyramid." These models can be adapted to other subjects in a school curriculum and will motivate students through innovative methods.

Public library programs address these ten new subjects as well. They go beyond the research and more academic boundaries of most school projects, but all programs include books and stories as a base. The related activities in the public library area will appeal to many ages and interests of children. Active kids will love "Australian animal acrobatics" and new twists on traditional relay games. Skit kits will excite theatrical children. Artistic children will become engrossed in making rainforest masks, Punch and Judy puppet theatres, paper castles, and friendship crafts. All kids will laugh at the humorous skit on manners or come to join their friends at a "Between Friends Party."

Annotated chapter bibliographies list a wide range of materials from picture books to longer fiction and nonfiction for all age and grade levels of elementary school. Some Web sites are also included throughout the chapters with a special focus on Web sites in the author biography chapter. Children can't seem to find enough biographical material about their favorite children's book authors and illustrators in book format. I have listed numerous Web sites that authors and their publishers have created to satisfy kids' curiosity.

May the hardworking teachers and children's librarians discover even more ways to share stories with young people today. We want kids to see meaning beyond Question 25 on the state standards test and to be inspired to express themselves more effectively than through the acronym phrases and emoticons we see in e-mails. Tomorrow's citizens depend on our efforts, as noted author Jane Yolen so wisely reminds us: "To do without tales and stories . . . is to lose humanity's past . . . to have no star map for the future."

Welcome to the Middle Ages

Welcome to the Middle Ages! Imagine that you are a ten-year-old boy in the year 2006. How easily can your mind slip back to the year A.D. 506, more than 1,500 years ago? What would be the first thoughts that come into your mind when your teacher announces you will be returning to the "Middle Ages"? If you are an eleven-year-old girl, would you imagine a world of courtship and castle adventures? Would you become excited like Josh or Emma in Bailey's book *Adventures in the Middle Ages* to go into a time warp and actually meet people from the past? Would you even have a general idea of what was going on during the sixth through the fourteenth or fifteenth centuries?

Children experience history in a different way from adults. They have a smaller frame compared with our own more expanded panoramic sense of time. After all, children have lived only a few short years themselves. Ask a class of fifth graders today what they remember about the year 2000 or the millennium events surrounding the shift from December 31, 1999, to January 1, 2000. Remember, a fifth grader today was only a preschool-age child at that time.

Most children in elementary school have some knowledge of the Middle Ages through having seen films and videos about King Arthur or reading fairytales about kings and queens during these times. Boys are drawn to books on medieval weapons, and girls often clamor for stories such as "Sleeping Beauty." Both sexes listen with interest to details about the Black Plague and what food was served at a medieval banquet. Because children are interested in these topics and have some previous knowledge, this subject will be an easy sell for teachers and librarians to explore further with young audiences.

The Middle Ages were fascinating times full of harrowing journeys on the Crusades to the Holy Lands, of local or national battles on horseback between knights in armor, of scary days when people died from gruesome diseases when the practice of medicine relied heavily on superstition and hocus pocus. People still believed the planets revolved around the earth and were afraid if they sailed too far that they might drop off the edge of the world. Within a few hundred years, many of these uninformed views would change radically. Studying the Middle Ages begins with a general understanding of history from approximately A.D. 500 to 1400 or 1500 and placing that time period in a larger context of events before and after that time. A study of any historical topic involves events, values, places, and people. In this case, students might learn about the Crusades and the Black Death (events), Feudalism and a knight's code of ethics (values), castles and buildings in a medieval village (places), bonesetters and wool merchants, knights and kings (people).

The librarian or teacher will need to decide the scope for studying such a vast topic. Will your unit become an in depth study of the Middle Ages culminating in a daylong Medieval Fair for sixth-grade students and their families? Will you, the school media specialist, show one fifth-grade class how to do research on the Middle Ages for a short paper? Or will you (classroom teacher or school librarian) simply wish to provide a little background on this time period in preparation for retelling a Saint George and the Dragon tale?

Children's librarians in public settings plan entertaining, educational programs. Their approach may overlap with school purposes, but generally they set a lighter tone. Medieval summer reading programs continue to be popular in public libraries all over the country. "Castle Quest," "Readers of the Round Table," and "Dragonsummer" represent the titles of some state summer reading programs in the United States. Children enjoy jousting demonstrations, making paper castles, and performing puppet shows with dragon marionettes while they read for reading incentive prizes. Other libraries hold annual medieval storytelling events during the winter months.

This chapter could easily become an entire book because so many resources are available on this topic, and the interest continues to grow. The length of the bibliography alone demonstrates the wealth of information available on the Middle Ages. I have selected some topics with projects and activities suitable for a school program. The topics and research are organized into subtopics such as "Government and the Feudal System" and "The Literary Scene."

Several individual assignments for each subtopic are provided. These assignments then become portions of group projects described next. I have also provided a pathfinder page to guide the student through researching the various topics, and I included a brief evaluation form for students to give positive comments to one another. Not all chapters are as lengthy as this, but this one is meant to be a model for planning units on other historical periods.

The public library program consists of stories and several hands-on projects. A buffet of medieval foods can be served, and children could come in costumes. One of the projects, a Punch and Judy puppet stage with small stick puppets, along with a short play, has been included, although most theatricals of this kind were performed after medieval times. The other projects focusing on a paper castle and illuminated letters replicate arts during the Middle Ages.

With numerous hands-on projects and topics to research, children will be able to gain a lively sense of the Middle Ages. No doubt this interest will continue throughout their lives given the number of books that continue to be published on the topic and the proliferation of historical reenactment groups flourishing in the United States.

Bibliography

Aliki. *A Medieval Feast.* HarperCollins, 1981.
> The lord of the manor at Camdenton prepares for a feast when the king and his entourage come to visit. Preparations include hunting, growing vegetables, making bread, and cooking the elaborate feast. Splendid dishes such as peacock, blackbird pie, and a castle-shaped pastry are served.

Bailey, Linda. *Adventures in the Middle Ages.* Illustrated by Bill Slavin. Kids Can Press, 2000.
> Emma and Josh open the pages of a time-travel guide to the Middle Ages that they find in an old bookstore. Upon opening the book, they are thrust into the Middle Ages, where they meet peasants and knights and learn about living in villages and castles.

Chaucer, Geoffrey. *Canterbury Tales.* Adapted by Barbara Cohen. Illustrated by Trina Schart Hyman. Lothrop, Lee & Shepard, 1988.
> Cohen selects four tales to retell in a spirited style for this beautiful collection. Trina Schart Hyman's carefully detailed illustrations work perfectly for this book.

Chaucer, Geoffrey. *The Canterbury Tales.* Retold by Geraldine McCaughrean. Puffin Books, 1997.
> About one dozen of Chaucer's tales are retold in modern English in a lively manner with a new narrative version of the famous prologue. This is a good version for older elementary students to the medieval classic.

Cole, Joanna. *Ms. Frizzle's Adventures: Medieval Castle.* Illustrated by Bruce Degen. Scholastic Books, 2003
     The beloved teacher and her students go down a trapdoor in a castle bookshop, don medieval costumes, and go on a trip to a medieval castle. They make friends with people from ages past, learn about life during the Middle Ages, experience a battle, and return to the bookshop.

Cushman, Karen. *Catherine, Called Birdy.* Clarion, 1994.
     Set during the Middle Ages, this story told in diary format tells about a thirteen-year-old daughter of an English knight. Catherine is frustrated with the usual expectations for a young woman and wants to be able to choose to marry or not. This spunky young heroine will appeal to young people of today.

Cushman, Karen. *Matilda Bone.* Clarion, 2000.
     Fourteen-year-old Matilda, raised and educated in a manor, is forced to make her way in the medieval world of bonesetting and practicing medicine rather than reading and contemplating ideas.

Cushman, Karen. *The Midwife's Apprentice.* Clarion, 1995.
     An unnamed girl who began life among dung heaps in fourteenth-century England learns the trade of midwifery thus advancing her station in life. In time, the waif receives a name and is accepted by Jane the Midwife, and "Alyce" finds food as well as a purpose for her life.

Daly-Weir, Catherine. *Coat of Arms.* Illustrated by Jeff Crosby. Grosset & Dunlap, 2000.
     Basic information about medieval knights is included in this book that gives detailed information about the color, design, and symbolism of coats of arm. Stencils and bold illustrations will help children wishing to design their own projects.

Dawson, Imogene. *Food and Feasts in the Middle Ages.* New Discovery Books, 1994.
     In this social history, menus and recipes for medieval foods are given along with explanations for why people ate certain foods and at what times of year special feasts were eaten. Plentiful colored illustrations of medieval paintings and maps accompany the informative text.

De Angeli, Marguerite. *The Door in the Wall.* Doubleday, 1949.
     A crippled boy in fourteenth-century England shows courage and is recognized by the king. This book won the Newbery Award in 1950.

Gibbons, Gail. *Knights in Shining Armor.* Little, Brown, 1995.
     One of Gibbons's especially informative books describes and illustrates parts of the castle complex, a knight's training, armor, and code of chivalry. This text is useful for basic research for elementary students.

Hart, Avery, and Paul Mantell. *Knights and Castles: 50 Hands-On Activities to Experience the Middle Ages.* Williamson, 1998.
     Extensive information about the Middle Ages in general and on many specialized topics such as games, plays, craft projects, and recipes appear in this well-formatted book. Children will be motivated to read and try out the wealth of ideas presented.

Hastings, Selina. *Sir Gawain and the Loathly Lady.* Illustrated by Juan Wijngaard. Mulberry Books, 1987.
     This famous legend tells the story of King Arthur who must answer a vital question of the Black Knight. An old hag agrees to help if Arthur promises to fulfill her fondest wish. The wish comes at a high price in that the hag asks to marry one of Arthur's knights. Gawain volunteers to help his king and marries the woman. Because Gawain treats her nobly and allows her to make her own choices,

the spell is broken. This legend is retold throughout literature, and the vital question is an important component in Chaucer's "Wife of Bath's Tale."

Hinds, Kathryn. *Life in the Middle Ages: The Castle.* Marshall Cavendish, 2001.

One in a series on the Middle Ages, this volume describes various topics on the subject of castle life including feudal fortresses, the roles of lords and ladies, tournaments, and festivities. Medieval paintings and prints in color add to the beauty of this detailed text for upper elementary students. Others in the series by Hinds: *The Church, The Countryside,* and *The City.*

Hodges, Margaret. *Merlin and the Making of the King.* Illustrated by Trina Schart Hyman. Holiday House, 2004.

Three stories are retold in this attractive shorter book. They are "The Sword in the Stone," "Excalibur," and "The Lady of the Lake." Merlin watches over the young Arthur in these stories.

Hodges, Margaret. *Saint George and the Dragon.* Illustrated by Trina Schart Hyman. Little, Brown, 1984.

In dramatic language, Hodges retells this classic legend of the Red Cross Knight who kills a dragon. Hodges used Spenser's *Fairie Queen* as a model. Hyman's powerful illustrations won the Caldecott Medal. Although the legend predates the Middle Ages, the idea of medieval chivalry grew from legends like this one.

Langley, Andrew. *Medieval Life.* Knopf, 1996.

In this Eye Witness book, topics include peasant life, the royal court, life in a monastery, a soldier's life, guilds, and entertainment. Numerous pictures and sidebars make the book appealing for a wide age range of children.

Lasker, Joe. *Merry Ever After.* Viking Press, 1976.

Two stories about medieval weddings are told. The first tells the elaborate preparations and festivities for a noble couple's wedding. The second contrasts sharply in describing the simple country wedding of a peasant couple. Text and jewel-toned illustrations contribute to an enchanting book.

McGovern, Ann. *If You Lived in the Days of the Knights.* Illustrated by Dan Andreasen. Scholastic, 2001.

Good basic information about the feudal system, training for knights, and design of castles is presented in a question-and-answer format. The book reads well for those curious about the subject and provides clear information for school reports.

Nikola-Lisa, W. *Till Year's Good End: A Calendar of Medieval Labors.* Illustrated by Christopher Manson. Atheneum, 1997.

This lavishly illustrated picture book traces farm activities throughout the calendar year during the Middle Ages in the manner of a Book of Hours. Although these medieval books actually illustrated the 365 feast days of the Church, this book uses two poetic lines for each month (January: "By the fire I warm my hands/And gaze upon yon frozen lands") then describes the activity pictured in the style of the period. The pen-and-ink and watercolor pictures are reminiscent of woodblock.

Platt, Richard. *Castle Diary: The Journal of Tobias Burgess.* Candlewick, 1999.

When eleven-year-old Toby is sent to be a page in his uncle's castle, the boy begins keeping a detailed journal. He writes about everything from baking bread to boar hunts and tournaments. Set in thirteenth-century England, the writing style is lively and will give children information as they become absorbed in the story. This book could be used as a companion to Cushman's *Catherine Called Birdy.*

Scieszka, Jon. *Knights of the Round Table.* Illustrated by Lane Smith. Viking, 1991.

In this Time Warp Trio book, Joe, Fred, and Sam are transported back to the Middle Ages through a magic wish card given to Joe by his Uncle Joe. The boys encounter the Black Knight and meet King Arthur, Guinevere, and some disgusting giants. In spite of all the fun, the boys want to return home and are assisted by Merlin's magic book, only to find themselves in trouble with Joe's mother when they arrive back where they started.

The Story of the Middle Ages: A School Program

This program plan is designed for a three- to four-week-long study of the Middle Ages, but it may be adapted for a shorter unit. It includes sequential steps for the teacher/media specialist in introducing the topic, guiding children through research, listing sample topics for short reports, and creating topics for group projects. A medieval fair can be held as a culminating activity.

Because of the broad scope of this topic, the librarian can work with teachers in various subject areas. For example, science teachers could contribute lessons on disease prevention, early astronomy, and growing medicinal herbs. A music teacher might play a medieval ballad, a recording of a chant, or teach children a round. An art teacher could show samples of medieval paintings. Math teachers might create medieval word problems using the Web site "Math for Kids: A Medieval Adventure in Problem-solving" (http://library.thinkquest.org/).

Materials Needed

Children will use their own materials for projects.

Food will be needed to make the feast according to your menu plans.

Procedure

Session 1

1. Teacher/media Specialist (teacher/m.s.) introduces the topic to children by reading a book such as Gail Gibbons's *Knights in Shining Armor* or Joanna Cole's *Ms. Frizzle's Adventures: Medieval Castle.*

2. Children ask questions with prompts from the teacher/m.s., who has set up a book display. Several books in the bibliography are set up in question-answer format to provide answer for teachers and students. *How Would You Survive in the Middle Ages?* is a particularly useful source. Students can use these resources to complete reports described in this chapter.

3. Teacher/m.s. distributes "report cards" (index cards with short assignments for students). Examples of these are included in this chapter.

Session 2

1. Students share their reports orally and in written form so that the teacher can photocopy them for class distribution. Teachers can duplicate the reports so that each student can compile individual medieval notebooks.

2. Teacher reads a chapter or portion of a chapter from one of the longer books listed in the bibliography. I recommend one of the shorter novels such as *Castle Diary.* If students are older, one of Karen Cushman's books would be a good choice.

Session 3

1. Students continue sharing their reports.

2. Teacher continues reading the longer book.

Session 4

1. Media specialist or teacher instructs students how to use reference sources to prepare for their final projects. The pathfinder included in this chapter will be useful for teachers and students. This library research tool defines a topic and guides the student in researching a topic. Typical search terms are given, as well as selective sources. Provide each student with a blank copy of this sheet.

2. Teacher/m.s. continues reading a longer book. If finished, another book may be read.

Session 5

1. Media specialist/teacher sets up displays (books, perhaps visuals such as maps or models of castles and calligraphy) and encourages children to browse.

2. Students select their term projects.

Sessions 6–10

1. Students work individually and in groups on their projects.

2. Teacher/m.s. continues reading longer books or works with students about report writing and researching.

3. Students write invitations to outside guests (family members or adult friends) to attend the Medieval Fair to be held on Session 15.

Sessions 11–14

1. Groups present their projects to one another. Note: These projects will be briefly explained and demonstrated at the Medieval Fair for parents during Session 15.

2. Teacher/m.s. asks students to evaluate the projects using the evaluation form provided.

Session 15: The Medieval Fair

1. Teacher/m.s. or students greet guests for the Medieval Fair. The "greeter" could dress as a town crier or a noble welcoming everyone to the day's festivities.

2. Each group gives a short summary of its project to the entire group. Then guests have an opportunity to visit each project center as they ask questions of the students.

3. Refreshments from the period are served and a story is read. A menu is provided in this chapter.

Student Reports: A Suggested List

Write out the assignments on large index cards or on full-sized 8 1/2 x 11 paper rolled into scrolls for a more authentic medieval touch. These short reports will be a first step to the final projects. The assignments are grouped in categories. You may, of course, adapt these topics for your students.

Government and the Feudal System

1. Research basic government structure during the Middle Ages. Each strata of the society was based on land ownership. This was known as the Feudal System. Each strata—royalty, the Church, nobles, knights, and peasants—had a place and served an important function for society as a whole. Briefly describe the importance of each. (You might assign a different student to describe each of these roles. Note that a separate category has been developed for knights and knighthood.)

2. Describe laws, trials, and punishments.

Knights and Knighthood

1. Clothing and armor of a knight: What kinds of armor might a knight use? Find pictures of various styles.

2. Weapons of the Middle Ages: What basic weapons were used by the individual knight and by the armies of knights? Find pictures.

3. Preparations for knighthood: What different stages might a young man undergo in becoming a knight? Describe chivalry and the knight's responsibility to the idea of chivalry.

4. Medieval battles: What was the outcome? What conflicts led up to the battle? Write a battle plan and also a resolution that might have prevented the conflict from becoming a battle.

Medieval Learning and Thinking

1. Knowledge of geography during the Middle Ages: What kingdoms and countries in Europe and the Middle East existed? What explorations took place between the years 500 and 1500?

2. Scientific knowledge of the heavens of this time period: What basic ideas were known in the area of astronomy?

3. Biological knowledge of this time period: What basic ideas were known in the medical and health field? Describe medical practitioners—including the duties of doctors, midwives, bonesetters, surgeons—and the use of herbs for medicinal use.

4. Engineering and technology of this time period: What basic technology was used in agriculture, communication, and warfare?

5. Education during this time period: Describe universities, schools, and training during the time. Describe what literacy would have meant during the Middle Ages.

Castle Life and Town Life

1. Castle life during the Middle Ages: Who would have lived in castles, and what were the general responsibilities of each kind of person (for example, the lady of the castle)?

2. Castle building: Find illustrations of a typical castle design. What was the purpose of each part of the castle (for example, the castle keep or the moat)?

3. Town life during this time period: Find illustrations of typical towns and the buildings from the Middle Ages.

Food and Banquets

1. Food of peasants in the Middle Ages: What foods were eaten, and how were they prepared? Include information about what crops farmers grew.

2. Hunting during the Middle Ages: Which animals were hunted and which animals were raised on farms for food during the Middle Ages? Find pictures of these animals and of medieval hunters.

3. Herbs grown to use in cooking during the Middle Ages: Find herb charts and pictures of typical herbs.

4. Castle kitchens and kitchen implements during the Middle Ages: Find pictures of the kitchens and the implements. Do a basic report on what foods were prepared in these kitchens. Find recipes for typical dishes.

5. Medieval banquets: What foods were served? How was food served? Find sample menus for those banquets.

6. Entertainment at the medieval banquet: What kind of performers might be present?

Guilds and the Arts during the Middle Ages

1. Guilds during this period: Why did guilds develop? How were guilds formed? What kinds of guilds existed during this time period? Be specific in naming these.

2. Fabric arts during this time period: Describe the spinning and weaving processes and describe what kinds of fabrics were made for household use.

3. Medieval tapestry art: Describe needlework, embroidery, and find pictures of famous tapestries of the period.

4. Medieval arts of painting and sculpture: Find examples of famous paintings and pieces of sculpture.

5. Art of calligraphy and illuminated manuscripts: Find examples of medieval writing and illuminated alphabets.

6. Medieval music: Find examples of musical instruments and songs of the Middle Ages.

The "Literary Scene"

1. Medieval legends and myths: Find several myths from this time period. Describe the basic story, the characters, and what you learned from these myths.

2. Find several legends about Arthur and his Knights of the Round Table. Retell one legend.

3. Find out about the writer Chaucer and briefly describe his tales. Select one tale to retell. Several good versions are retold for children, such as Selina Hastings's *The Canterbury Tales: A Selection,* and Cohen's *Canterbury Tales.*

4. News events during any year between 500 and 1500: What subjects might be covered if you were to write a newspaper for the times? Write one article for this newspaper.

Term Projects: A Selected List

The following list proposes several group projects for the final term projects. These activities are expansions of the topics listed under the Student Reports section.

Medieval Government and the Feudal System

Recreate each basic level of a medieval society under feudalism for your group presentation. You might make charts, write a script, or create a story to introduce a king, noble, church bishop, knight, lord, lady, and peasants.

If you choose to write a story, you'll want to think of action so each character can participate. (The book *Merry Ever After* tells about two weddings, one noble and one peasant. This story could be retold.)

Include your earlier reports and any visuals to help other students understand the government structure during this time period.

Knights and Knighthood

Show how boys prepared for knighthood. Then assume the role of a knight and describe your plans for a upcoming battle.

Make a display board or display table with posters and charts to describe weapons, armor, and clothing for knights.

Medieval Learning

Assume you are a team of medieval scholars. The king calls on you when a series of disasters happen in the realm. A mysterious disease is spreading throughout the land. Crops are in danger, people are becoming ill, and a nearby kingdom is threatening war.

Write a script to tell this situation to the other groups in your classroom with different members of your group taking parts to give the king advice what to do about dealing with these events.

Create a display table or display board to show what was known in the fields of geography, medical science, astronomy, and technology at the time as part of your group's project.

Castle Life and Town Life

Build a model castle and explain through charts and posters the function of each castle part.

Make a replica of a typical town in the Middle Ages. Describe the buildings and people who would have lived in those buildings.

Food and Banquets

Plan a medieval banquet for a noble or royalty during the Middle Ages. Create a menu, plans the foods, how much food you will need to prepare for a group of fifty people from different levels of society who might attend this banquet. Where and how will the guests be seated? Plan the entertainment and be prepared to set the tables properly.

Make a visual display, prepare several dishes of food at home to bring to school so that every class member will have a sample. Designate some class members in your group to perform an entertainment. You might retell a story or use a script in this chapter.

Guilds and the Arts

Designate different members of your group as members of typical guilds of the times. All guild members need to describe their work and demonstrate how they perform their jobs. The artists—painters, calligraphers, musicians, and so on—could create a work of art to show in your display.

The Literary Scene

Create a newsletter for one year and write articles for at least five different topics of interest of the day. Read some of your newsletter aloud and tell students how you gathered your news. In addition, the minstrels or storytellers introduce their legends and stories and retell them orally to the class.

The Medieval Fair

At the end of this unit, stage a medieval fair for parents and guests. Each project group sets up its display and describes its project for approximately five minutes. Because time is limited, students will need to summarize the project very briefly. The performing groups such as the storytellers may be given a little more time to do their oral presentations.

Pathfinder for Researching the Middle Ages

Definition of the Middle Ages: The Middle Ages, or medieval times, were a period of history lasting about one thousand years from approximately A.D. 400 when the Roman Empire fell until about 1400 to 1500 when the Renaissance began.

General Encyclopedias to Use: *World Book Encyclopedia*
(List other encyclopedias in your school in written or electronic form.)

General Reference Sources on the Middle Ages (see bibliography of this chapter to include a few titles):

Search Terms to Use for General Study:

The Middle Ages

Medieval

Knights and Castles

(Add your own.)

Your Specific Topic Area: (Student fills this out. For example: "Knights and Knighthood" or "Castle Life and Town Life in the Middle Ages.")

Specific Books and Selected Materials You Find: (Students fill this out using Internet sites, books from the bibliography in this chapter, books they find from your school or public library.)

Evaluation Form for Students

Please evaluate your peers by giving them positive feedback and suggestions about their reports. Remember, you appreciate good suggestions and encouragement. Do this for others.

Title of Report:

Name or names of students you are evaluating:

Most effective part of this report:

One suggestion that might improve this report:

Supportive comment (positive):

Your Name:

The Medieval Banquet Menu

Medieval diets varied considerably. Basically city dwellers ate more elaborately than country dwellers, and nobles ate more elaborately than peasants. Menus focused around a roast or stewed meat with several other courses for those who could afford the variety. Fresh fruits and vegetables such as salad greens were served, and dessert might consist of a light cake and sweet wine.

Banquets for royalty became showcases for such fancies as peacocks (feathers were plucked when the birds were roasted, then the plumage was reassembled to serve), game birds encased in gold, and whole suckling pigs. Cakes might be made in the shape of a wild animal. This was truly a "meal fit for a king"!

Sample medieval menus listed some food in terms unfamiliar to the modern cook. These include "pottage," which was a kind of soup. "Pasties" were little pastries with meat filling; the term is still used in parts of Great Britain, and the food is served in pubs. Medieval diets consisted of many kinds of fowl that we still eat today, such as capon and chicken, but it also included doves and pigeons.

For your medieval fair, the following menu adaptations will be easier to use than those found in traditional medieval cookbooks.

Medieval Menu Suggestions for Today's Kids

Beef stew with onions and carrots, flavored with garlic and herbs (but no potatoes because they had not been introduced from the New World at that time)

Roast chicken with lemon

Grilled fish (trout or cod) seasoned with fresh parsley and sage

Cheese pie (similar to today's quiche; use a pastry crust and fill with cream cheese, parsley, oregano, eggs, salt, and pepper or consult a cookbook for another recipe

Stuffed eggs (hardboiled eggs with a little grated Swiss cheese, chopped parsley, and mustard added to the mashed egg yolk)

Rice pudding

Bread pudding with dried cherries or raisins

Fresh or dried fruits: melon, pears, strawberries, oranges, apples, grapes

Fresh green salad (Use field greens or spinach rather than head lettuce and dress with olive oil and vinegar, salt and pepper, and other fresh herbs as you like.)

Coarse bread such as a whole-grain wheat

Apple cider or grape juice

Library Castle Adventures: A Public Library Program

Children's librarians in public libraries can stage this program lasting about one to one and a half hours after school or on a Saturday for elementary school–age children. I recommend advertising the program as specifically suited to school-age children because the projects are beyond the understanding of preschoolers.

This program consists of reading or telling one or more stories selected from the bibliography and setting up plenty of tables for children to make the craft projects.

Materials Needed

1. Poster board or fabric to make banners and coats of arm if desired

2. Card stock or heavier paper for paper castles and puppet theatres

3. A large box of craft sticks for puppets

4. Several tape dispensers and multiple pairs of scissors

5. Fine-tipped colored markers and colored pencils for illuminated letters

6. Refreshments (ginger ale, oranges, and apples) for treats

Procedure

1. Before children come to the program, decorate the room with banners, shields with coat of arms, and any other memorabilia you can find.

2. Play recorded music from the period or invite musicians such as Celtic harp players to provide background music if desired.

3. When children arrive, greet them with a hearty "Welcome! Wassail! Here's to your health! Welcome to today's Library Castle Adventure!"

4. Read one or more stories to set the tone for a medieval program.

5. Instruct children to move to one of the craft tables to make the various projects. These projects include the following: Build Your Own Castle, Create a Fancy Medieval Letter, and Make Your Own Punch and Judy Theatre and Players.

6. Serve simple treats such as fruit and ginger ale or set out a more elaborate spread using the ideas in the school program feast.

Punch and Judy for Today's Children

Explain to children that Punch and Judy puppets in the past fought and mistreated one another in ways we find unacceptable today. Even the puppet play that appears here is not a model for good behavior, but puppets on a stage are allowed to act differently. We know they are merely playacting, and, in the end, no one really gets hurt. This same kind of "make-believe" fighting can be seen in *Roadrunner* cartoons in which victims might be run over by a steamroller but quickly recover. People laugh with the knowledge that this is only pretend.

Punch and Judy

Characters: Mr. Punch, Judy (his wife), their baby, and the Beadle or Constable, an officer of the law

Scene One

Punch: Judy!
(No answer)
Judy, my lass. Judy! Judy! Judy!
(She appears.)

Judy: That's my name. Don't wear it out!

Punch: Aye, that's my pretty wife.

Judy: And who are you?

Punch: Me? Punch!
(She slaps him.)
What ya doin' that for?

Judy: It's all your fault. You said, "Punch."

Punch: But that's my name. Punch.
(She slaps him again.)
Stop that! If you do that one more time, I'll punch you.

Judy: You are a mean man. I don't see why I put up with you.

Punch: Oh, Judy, my lass. Let us not quarrel. Give me a kiss.
(She slaps him.)
Now why did you punch me this time?

Judy: It's your fault.

Punch: Why?

Judy: You said to punch you in the kisser.

Punch: I did not say that! *(To audience)* I did not say that, did I?
Listen up, Judy. I want to start all over again. Let's be friends.

Judy: Why should we be friends?

Punch: Because we have a sweet little baby. Judy, bring me the baby.

Judy: Promise me you'll be good.

Punch: I promise.

Scene Two

Punch: Where is that woman? *(To audience)* Look, will you help me? Would you call out "Judy"? I don't want to get in trouble with that difficult wife of mine again. Come on, call out.
(Audience calls "Judy," and she appears with the baby.)

Judy: *(To audience)* Hello there. Have you seen Mr. Punch?
(Audience responds.)
Where is he? Oh, I see he is there.
Mr. Punch, can I trust you to be nice to the baby?

Punch: Just as sweet as my name,
Punch.
(She starts to hit him.)
Please, Judy, do not strike me. How can I help it if a have a silly name?
Now, give me the baby!
(Judy gives him the baby. She leaves, and the baby starts to cry.)

Punch: Oh dear! What shall I do? I know! I'll sing to the baby.
(Singing) Rock-a-bye Baby. *(Rocks baby. It stops crying.)*
There, that's better.
(Singing) Rock-a-bye Baby. Hmm, I can't remember the rest. *(To audience)*
Do you know the next line?
(Audience responds.)
Oh, yes, In the tree top/When the wind blows, the cradle will rock.
(He sings this and rocks baby.) What's next? *(Thinking)* Oh, yes!
(Singing) When the bough breaks/the cradle will fall
And down will come baby/cradle and all.
(He rocks baby very hard and drops baby down behind the stage. Baby screams.)
(Judy appears and is angry.)

Judy: I knew I couldn't trust you. You've thrown the baby away. I'm going to get the Beadle.
(She leaves.)

Scene Three

(Beadle appears on stage.)

Beadle: Where is that terrible man? Mr. Punch, I'm coming to take you down.
(Punch appears.)

Punch: Take me down? Who are you to take me down? And where are you taking me down?

Beadle: I am the Beadle.

Punch: You don't look like a beetle. You don't look like a bug!

Beadle: I am *NOT* a bug. I am the Beadle, the constable, an officer of the law.

Punch: Oh, I see. Well where do you think you're taking the likes of me?

Beadle: To the pokey.

Punch: The pokey? The Hokey Pokey? The dance hall?

Beadle: No, man! The pokey, the jail!

Punch: For what?

Beadle: I don't like you. Besides, you insulted me. You threw away the baby. And you are not very smart.

Punch: Sorry, sir. But I can't help bein' the way I am. Besides, I was only singing to the baby. She just jumped out of my arms. She's just like her mother, a little brat.
(Judy appears.)

Judy: You see what I told you, officer? Punch is impossible.

Officer: What shall I do with him?

Punch: Have mercy, sir. I love my Judy.

Beadle: He loves you! Can't you give him another chance?

Judy: Another chance? Well, if he promises to find the baby.

Punch: I do. I promise. I will.
(Punch exits.)

Beadle: Goodbye, Judy. I think this will all work out. But, my dear, you will have to promise to stop hitting the poor man. Will you do that?

Judy: *(Beadle exits. Punch reappears with baby.)* Very well.

Punch: Here is our baby, dear Judy. Could we kiss and make up now?

Judy: Oh, I suppose so. But only one little kiss.
(Punch kisses her three times.)

Judy: Oh, heavens. The man is trying to kill me with kindness. It's time to end this show before we get into another fight. Say good-bye, Mr. Punch.

Punch: Goodbye Mr. Punch.

Judy: You are a noodlehead. I guess I'll have to speak for both of us. *(To audience)* Goodbye, good audience. It's time to go home now. This ends our little show.

Art for Middle Ages

Castle Art

Make a three-dimensional paper castle by cutting out four tower sections and two gate sections of the castle pattern (Figure 1.1). Paint or color the castle sections first and draw in other details such as bars on gates and windows. Tape or glue two tower sections together to form longer sides to your castle. The front gate section is then glued to this long side, and another gate section becomes the back gate section when glued into place. Fold as indicated on the pattern before you glue. You may wish to enlarge this pattern.

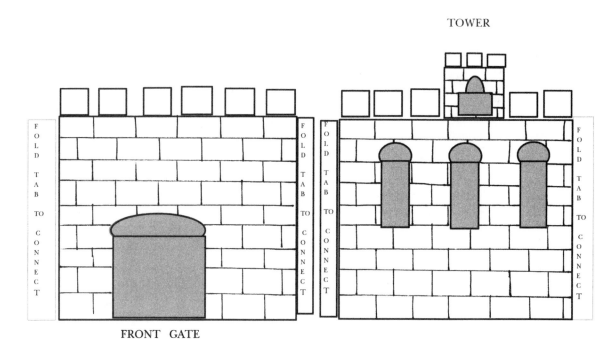

CASTLE

Figure 1.1

Medieval Illuminated Letters

Photocopy the entire alphabet outlines for each child (Figure 1.2). Provide markers, colored pencils, or paints for children to add details to the alphabet letters. Also photocopy the "O is for Owl" page so that children will be able to visualize how to make a fancy illuminated letter. Encourage children to draw their own favorite letters and add elaborate details.

Figure 1.2a

Figure 1.2b

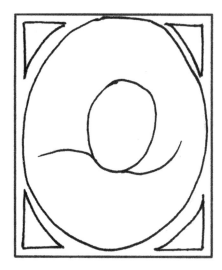

Figure 1.2c

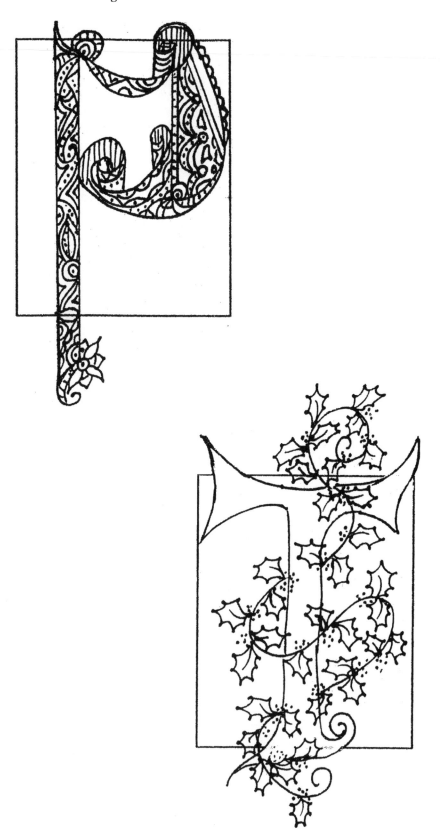

Figure 1.2d

Punch and Judy Theatre and Players.

Photocopy one center stage section (Figure 1.3a) and two plain side sections (Figure 1.3b) of the theatre for each child. Give children markers or colored pencils to decorate their stages. Instruct them to cut out the sections and fold on the dotted lines. Glue or tape the center stage and two wings together.

Carefully cut out the blank center of the center section so that the little puppets will be visible when they are manipulated behind this opening. Color the set of puppets—Punch, Judy, the baby, and the Constable or Beadle (Figure 1.4). Cut these out, leaving a little white border around the edges as the details may be lost if cut out too close to the edges. Tape a craft stick to the back of each figure with the stick attached to the top of each puppet. In this way, the puppeteer can lower and raise the puppet down to the opening in the stage.

Two people will be needed to do the play if one person manipulates the puppets and another reads the script provided in this chapter.

Figure 1.3a

FOLD

FOLD

Figure 1.3b

Figure 1.4

2

A Glimpse of Tropical Rainforests

How can children begin to grasp the enormity of a tropical rainforest? When we tell eight- or nine-year-old children that once 6 billion acres of forests covered the center of the globe but today less than 2.5 billion acres of rainforest remain, how can they visualize the vast loss? How can this world so far away become alive for today's children in the continental United States? And how can one chapter in a small resource book adequately discuss such a huge topic?

Obviously, the scope of one chapter can only provide a glimpse or overview of this exotic world for teachers, librarians, and children to explore through further study and activities. A bibliography of resources and two programs appropriate for public library and school programs are included. Sample topics for student work, original stories and scripts, as well as arts projects add to the chapter's interest. Children are fascinated with this topic, and it provides a natural path to a child's growing understanding of our natural world.

Tropical rainforests may be thousands of miles away from our homes, but children eagerly want to know more about them. Perhaps because this place *is* so different from our more familiar prairies, rocky coastlands, and plains, children pour over pictures of yellow-billed toucans and scarlet macaws found in rainforest canopies. A child may have caught numerous American bullfrogs in the spring, but secretly wishes one day to really see a red poison dart frog. Even if that child never travels to the Amazon, the excellent photographs in children's books and through dozens of Web sites open up fantastic views we can visit from our homes and libraries.

Although the monumentality of the Amazon rainforest may be too great for us to truly fathom, hands-on activities and materials can provide size comparisons. For example, small drawings of geckos shown in a child's hand in the Dorling Kindersley's book *Rain Forest* help children visualize this tiny lizard. Make life-size puppets of fruit bats and toucans. With your arms outstretched, compare this distance to the wingspan of a harpy eagle. (Assuming you are five feet tall, your wingspan would be five feet. If you invite a seven-foot-tall person to your library, his "wingspan" would compare with that of a harpy eagle. More than likely, you'll not know such a tall person, but kids would be fascinated by this sight!) Measure a fifty-foot length of twine to show the distance a gibbon can leap. Stretch out the twine on the floor so that children can measure the distance of their leaps in comparison.

Set the scene for your own classroom or library rainforest with an opened green umbrella or a huge mural displayed on the wall. Invite children to do research to define a tropical rainforest and their locations around the world. They will find out the rainforest is a place receiving eighty inches or more rain in one year. Put a blue mark on the wall to show this height. Tropical rainforests are found at the middle of the globe (the equator) and stretch between two imaginary lines of the Tropic of Cancer and Tropic of

Capricorn where the tropics can be found. Show these on a globe or map. To simulate the humid environment, use the rainforest visualization activity found in this chapter.

Basic information about rainforest layers, deforestation, its effects on wildlife and people, identifying animal and plant groups unique to rainforests as well as enumerating the medicines and products important to the rest of the world are but a few of the topics students will want to research. Refrain from assigning the typical written or oral report. In the spirit of this chapter, think of lively exercises and projects that make a much greater impact on children than a bland recitation of facts. Further, children will begin to think more creatively and discover ways to capture the attention of adults, news media, and government officials.

There are two complete programs for this chapter, one with unusual research topics that school media specialists and teachers can adapt for their science studies. When first planning workshops for teachers over eight years ago, I found a wealth of books on the topic. In updating that research for this book, I have been disappointed to find that fewer titles have been published recently. Children are still interested in the topic, and rainforests are studied in many public schools. I hope that the bibliography provided, along with Web sites and ideas in this chapter, will assist the curious educator.

The other program, "Explore a Tropical Rainforest," for public libraries focuses on several hands-on craft projects and story sharing. This "educational" subject holds so much fascination for children that public libraries will find it an appealing area for their programs as well. In fact, many libraries have created whole summer reading programs on this topic and have opened the eyes of children and parents to the wonders of other places in our world.

Bibliography

Albert, Toni. *The Remarkable Rainforest: An Active-Learning Book for Kids.* Illustrated by Ada Hanlon. Trickle Creek Books, 2nd ed., 2003.

This journey by the author and her husband through a tropical rainforest contains worksheets, quizzes, craft projects, games, and recipes. It is a valuable resource for teachers and librarians setting up programs and projects on this topic.

Brett, Jan. *The Umbrella.* Putnam's, 2004.

In this narrative, Carlos leaves his umbrella at the base of a large tree while he climbs up the tree. He is looking for animals who, in the meantime, crawl one by one into his umbrella until it is filled to overflowing. The animals all spill out; Carlos climbs down from the tree and wonders what happened to the animals. Brett's glorious illustrations bring the splendors of a rainforest alive, and the story makes a good read-aloud choice.

Cherry, Lynne. *The Great Kapok Tree: A Tale of the Amazon Rain Forest.* Harcourt Brace Jovanovich, 1990.

This modern classic rainforest story of two men who go into a tropical rainforest to cut down trees becomes a moving tale of various animals speaking to one of the men in his dream. They convince him that destroying even one tree would change their lives and upset the balance of life. This poignant story begs to be reenacted and will inspire children to write their own rainforest accounts.

Cunningham, Antonia. *Rainforest Wildlife.* Usbourne, 1993.

Brief sections on topics such as "Inside the Rainforest," "The Rainforest at Night," and "Birds of the Rainforest" describe the inhabitants of a tropical rainforest in succinct text and with numerous vivid illustrations.

Gibbons, Gail. *Nature's Green Umbrella: Tropical Rain Forests.* Morrow Junior, 1994.

Basic information about tropical rainforests includes numerous maps as well as diagrams showing the layers of a rainforest and what kinds of flora and fauna live in those layers. An explanation of this ecosystem and why it is endangered are included.

Guiberson, Brenda Z. *Rain, Rain, Rainforest.* Illustrated by Steve Jenkins. Holt, 2004.

This journey through a tropical rainforest captures the feeling of the wet, humid environment and introduces various animals that live there. The sounds and habits of each animal from sloths and salamanders to frogs, birds, and insects are vividly described. Jenkins's collage illustrations use unusual papers and textures to convey the unusual sights.

Hess, Paul. *Rainforest Animals.* Zero to Ten, 1996.

These short animal verses are fun for children to read aloud as they take a trip through the rainforest journey in this book.

Lewis, Scott. *The Rainforest Book.* Living Planet Press, 1990.

Among the topics included are deforestation and how to exert economic pressure on companies that profit from the destruction of the forests. Robert Redford wrote the book's preface.

Lyman, Francesca, compiler. *Inside the Dzanga-Sangha Rain Forest.* Workman, 1998.

This unusual book grew out of a research project for the American Museum of National History. The scientists, artists, and filmmakers who went to an African rainforest for six weeks returned to the United States to build a special exhibit of this rainforest. The book contains plenty of information about the rainforest, its structure, and the different forms of life contained in this ecosystem.

Nicholson, Sue. *Rainforest Explorer.* Tangerine Press, 2001.

This fascinating book is set up as if the reader is planning to go to the Amazon rainforest. Supply lists and preliminary information are provided. The rest of the book is written as a nature journal for a twelve-day exploration. Numerous full-color photographs and details will help children as they do the various projects in this chapter.

Parker, Edward. *Rain Forest Mammals.* Raintree Steck-Vaughn, 2003.

Some of the subtopics in this book include the diversity of mammals, lifestyles, and disappearing mammals. The author examines changes in the rainforest areas of the world by comparing these ecosystems as they were five hundred years ago with how they are today.

Pratt, Kristin Joy. *A Walk in the Rainforest.* Dawn, 1992.

Presented in an alphabetical arrangement, animals and plants living in a tropical rainforest are described and illustrated in brilliantly painted pictures. Factual information accompanies the main text lines.

Taylor, Barbara. *Rain Forest.* Dorling Kindersley, 1992.

Various animals and plants from a tropical rainforest are described in brief text and with amazingly clear photographs that show each example in its actual size. Helpful drawings show many of the animals in relationship to people. For example, a small praying mantis is shown on a human hand, and a dart frog is shown on top of a man's shoe. This close-up approach helps children understand sizes of these unusual life forms.

Take a Trip through a Tropical Rainforest: A School Program

This program simulates a trip through a rainforest with its learning centers, displays, reports, and activities. In preparation for the trip, invite your budding artists to turn the room into a rainforest setting. See the section "Rainforest Art" for ideas. Students research various topics and contribute to a simulated trip, resulting in a series of learning centers or displays set up around the library. A tour notebook filled with student pages in the form of stories, pamphlets, artwork, and so on is displayed so that this tour becomes a self-guided trip for visitors. In addition, the librarian could invite children to participate in a rainforest poem-writing contest. See the section "Write a Rainforest Poem" for details.

The elementary school curriculum often includes a rainforest segment, so the ideas here may be adapted as supplemental material for your own needs. This tour is planned for a school media center, but the ideas could be adapted for an individual classroom. Depending on the school calendar, this program could be a week- or even month-long program. Several grades could contribute to the learning centers and displays. For example, Grade 4 could be responsible for the first and last topics in this list, and Grades 5 and 6 could cover the other topics as listed.

Topics for student assignments are displayed in an inviting manner. The media specialist/librarian attaches to the library walls large sheets of paper or poster board in bright colors with titles on each board and gummed notes with various assignments. Creative "assignments" are suggested so that students will be inspired to think beyond the typical "report." For example, the topic "Animals in the Emergent Layer" might have notes such as these: "You are a harpy eagle. Tell your life story through words and illustrations. You might write a short biography or diary." "Study the life and habits of the blue morpho butterfly in preparation for your trip to the Amazon rainforest. Report your findings for the library tour."

Students make their selections by removing a gummed note and by signing the librarian's master list. The library media specialist also places a loose-leaf notebook on a worktable for students to add their pages to the Trip Guide. Further procedures for this tour program follow.

Materials Needed

1. Several rolls of brown wrapping paper and large sheets of green paper

2. Colored tissue paper for butterflies

3. Monkey and bird hand puppets (borrowed, if possible)

Procedure

1. The media specialist explains to students that they will be taking a trip through a tropical rainforest staged in the library media center. The introductory statement provided in this chapter could be part of the librarian's remarks. The media specialist then invites students to select the topics of their choice from the lists on the walls. The major topics to include are as follows:

   • Trip Plans

   • Introducing the Tropical Rainforest and Rainforest Concerns

   • Plant and Animal Life in the Rainforest Emergent Layer

   • Plant and Animal Life in the Rainforest Canopy

   • Plant and Animal Life in the Rainforest Understory

   • Plant and Animal Life on the Rainforest Floor

Students make their choices and sign the master list.

2. In the days or weeks that follow, students research their topics in the library media center with guidance from the librarian. Prepare a rainforest pathfinder if desired using the pathfinder model described in Chapter 1, "Welcome to the Middle Ages."

3. Encourage students to collect realia, make drawings, select library books, and print photographs from the Internet to make the display part of this project more visually appealing. Students will also prepare a page or two for the Tour Notebook. This notebook will be a written guide for those who take the self-guided tour of the library rainforest.

4. The library media specialist and classroom teachers read stories and do interactive exercises with children throughout the course of this unit.

5. Students bring their completed work to the library media center and assemble materials on one of the learning center tables. Some students may need wall space to display maps, posters, or large charts.

6. A special day or week may be scheduled for students to view the library media center "virtual" tour. Parents and guests are invited to come as well as all classes in the school.

    Sample topics for poster boards are as follows.

Trip Plans

Plan 1:

You are in charge of buying supplies for taking photographs, keeping notes, and doing research on the trip. Make a supply list and research where you can find these materials. Gather samples, catalogues, Web sites, and so on.

Plan 2:

As the medical advisor of this trip, research which diseases you might encounter in the rainforest. Be prepared to inform the team about these and what preventive measures should be taken.

Plan 3:

As the transportation and geographic guide, you will need to find maps of tropical rainforests in the Amazon area. Research transportation you will take to arrive in the area and the transportation needed once you're there.

Rainforest Introduction and Concerns

Tour Guide:

As the tour guide, you are responsible for informing the team about rainforests. Assume we know very little. Provide basic info. Create posters, brochures, trivia questions, or anything you think might be helpful.

Word Master:

How can we know what all those words such as "deforestation" and "biome" mean? Design a word game or illustrated glossary to help us.

Rainforest Concerns:

You have just founded an organization to protect tropical rainforests. Communicate the problems to the public by writing an editorial or by designing a flyer asking for donations to protect rainforests.

Life in the Emergent Layer

Example One:

You are a harpy eagle. Tell your life story using words and pictures. Use diary form or a first-person narrative story.

Example Two:

You are a scientist preparing to study blue morpho butterflies in a rainforest. Report your findings.

Example Three:

Select three interesting plants or animals found in the emergent layer. Tell the team about these and how they survive.

Life in the Canopy

Example One:

You are a medical researcher looking for plants that have been important for medicinal extracts. Which plants that grow in the canopy could be tested for improving health? Report your findings in a notebook.

Example Two:

Choose a kind of monkey or frog that lives in the canopy and write a news article for a children's science magazine about them. Include a picture of your animal.

Example Three:

Describe two or three kinds of birds that live in the canopy. Your descriptions could be written in a factual report form or as a science museum brochure copy. Add drawings or photographs.

Life in the Understory

Example One:

You are a spider monkey living in the understory. Describe the view of the world from where you live. What other animals do you see from the canopy above and the floor below?

Example Two:

You are an artist who has been hired to do a mural of the understory. You only need to paint the plants (trees, vines, flowers). Other artists will paint the animals. Paint or draw your mural and label each kind of plant.

Example Three:

Write a story about the sloth. Research carefully so your story details will be accurate.

Life on the Rainforest Floor

Anteater Antics:

A book publisher has hired you to do a short nonfiction book about anteaters. Research this topic and prepare a book outline with chapter headings then write an introduction to the book for the publisher.

Insects on the Floor:

Choose two insects that live on the rainforest floor. Describe their lives and how they view the rainforest from this place. Write your ideas in the form of a story or a diary.

Walking through the Rainforest:

Imagine you have poor vision as you are walking through the rainforest. Describe the sounds and smells of the rainforest. Use details so other visually impaired people can understand life in this world.

Rainforest Art: Room Display Ideas

Do you have unsightly pillars or columns in your library? They can be covered with wrinkled brown wrapping paper to simulate tree trunks. Add large, green leaf cutouts at the top. Position tissue paper butterflies on the trees at different heights. Hang monkey and bird puppets from the ceiling of the room for a simple but inviting rainforest recreation.

Invite young artists to paint the walls of the library with rainforest murals by stretching long sheets of brown wrapping paper or rolls of art paper along the walls. Display some of the beautifully illustrated books listed in the bibliography to give artists' ideas of a rainforest environment.

Write Your Own Rainforest Poem

Hold a Rainforest Poem Writing Contest in your library or school. Sarah Weeks's poem and songs in *Crocodile Smile* and Joanne Ryder's poetic text in *Jaguar in the Rainforest* can be displayed along with other books of nature or haiku poetry for inspiration.

If you want to provide some structure to this activity, you could give children a title such as "Rainforest Home" or "World Watch." You might write an opening line for children to finish. "Sing to the Rainforest/Don't Let It Go ..."

Collect all poems for a bulletin board display, a final published booklet to distribute, or for a read-aloud rainforest night at your library or school.

Explore a Tropical Rainforest: A Public Library Program

This program will provide ideas for an afternoon or after-school program lasting about an hour and a half. Elementary school–age children are the target audience, although the ideas work with middle school children as well. Because of the popularity of this topic, some public libraries have used the rainforest theme for an entire summer reading program quite successfully. Decorate the library with vines and a canopy of brightly colored animal figures. Frame the entrance to the children's area with pots of real bromeliad. Plan programs with featured guests who have traveled to rainforests. The following plan may be adapted as librarians wish.

Materials Needed

1. Tan or green twine for vines

2. Rainforest puppets or stuffed animals as desired

3. Bromeliad plants if desired

4. Photocopies of masks

5. Elastic cording (twelve inches per mask for each child)

6. Photocopies of birds and bats or seven poster boards in the following colors: red, orange, pink, yellow, green, blue, and black

7. Craft sticks or seven paint sticks

8. Photocopies of animals for "The Finest Flying Frog"

Procedure

1. Create a rainforest setting simply or elaborately as time and resources permit. Hang green twine that is knotted and twisted from the ceiling or opening to the children's room of the library. Display puppets or stuffed animals of rainforest animals around the room. Monkeys, parrots, snakes, eagles, butterflies, and toucans make perfect choices.

2. Set up tables for the arts projects, an area for storytelling and story reenactments. Provide a cart or table for refreshments.

3. Create a rainforest mood by playing an audiotape of rainforest sounds as children arrive. Then begin the program by reading or using words of your own similar to the "Rainforest Guided Imagery" description found later in this chapter. Play the rainforest game described later in this chapter.

4. Read one or two of the books listed in the bibliography. *The Umbrella* and *The Great Kapok Tree* are excellent stories for a wide audience.

5. After reading *The Great Kapok Tree,* tell children they may take part in retelling the story. I suggest using your own words in this way.

    Once a man went into the Amazon rainforest with an ax under his arm. The rainforest was hot—so hot that he continually wiped his brow of sweat. He looked around briefly, then swung his ax, striking the trunk of a tree in front of him. After a few strokes, the man felt very drowsy. He put down his ax, sat down at the base of the tree, and quickly fell asleep. In his sleep, voices called to him. [Instruct children to come up to the man, one by one, to warn him of the dangers of cutting down the tree. Each child or group of children take the roles of different rainforest animals that appear in Cherry's book. Older children will be able to create longer dialogue. Younger children may simply say to the man, "Señor, I am an anteater (or some other animal), please do not cut down this tree. It is my home."]

    [After all children have assembled around the sleeping man, open your eyes and say:] The man awoke from his dream. He saw the beauty of all the creatures from the rainforest around him. He was amazed. Then he picked up his ax and thoughtfully walked out of the rainforest.

6. Direct children to one of the craft tables to make the following projects:

    • Rainforest masks—see examples in this chapter (Figures 2.1–2.3).

    • Rainforest stick puppets—use patterns in this chapter (Figures 2.4–2.5).

    Enlarge patterns so that the puppets will be generously sized, at least as large as a piece of construction paper. If you can afford it, purchase enough poster board for each child to have a half sheet, because puppets approximately 11 x 14 inches are much more showy if you plan to use them in a dramatic reenactment. Note: These stick puppets will be used in retelling the stories during this program. Children may take them home to decorate their rooms at home, too.

7. Direct children to participate in the original stories "The Bat" and "The Finest Flying Frog in the Jungle" in this chapter.

8. Serve rainforest treats. Make rainforest banana splits with bananas cut into spears served with orange sherbet or vanilla ice cream and chopped nuts on top. Children who are allergic to nuts or ice cream could be served bananas dipped in a cinnamon-sugar mixture then skewered on a wooden stick.

9. At the end of the program, the librarian may want to inspire kids to become "rainforest activists" to preserve rainforest of the world. Pass out the "Rainforest Action Sheet' to those who are interested. This handout appears at the end of this chapter.

Rainforest Game

Using a rainforest rhyme (a sample follows), invite children to join in by naming a different animal for each letter of the alphabet. Use the game as a transition between activities or in another context, such as ending the day's work.

Rainforest Rhyme

> *In the rainforest*
> *Come to see*
> *Animals with names*
> *From A to Z.*

When the group is unable to come up with an answer for a particular letter, write that letter down to think about later. These unanswered responses will lead kids to research the Internet for unusual answers!

Rainforest Guided Imagery

Note: Use this mood-setting passage to begin the "Explore a Tropical Rainforest" program or whenever you want to settle children down after an intense activity. Subdue the light level in the room to help create a relaxing pace and speak in a slower, lower tone of voice.

Please close your eyes. Imagine you are in a place that is hot and wet. The air is heavy, thick with the smell of rotting leaves and sweet flowers. You feel very warm and sleepy. You do not drift into sleep because sounds fill the air everywhere around you.

Insects buzz, birds screech and call to each other. A bat whooshes by. Or is it a large bird? Do not open your eyes to see. Try to imagine what is around you through closed eyes. Trees taller than your house or apartment building surround you. In those branches you can hear monkey chatter. Creatures with claws and tails jump from limb to limb. They may be leaping jaguars. Listen carefully. That very, very slow tread above you could be a lumbering sloth, the slowest creature in the world. Though you cannot see the sloth, you can smell it. Sloths move so slowly that algae grows all over their backs. Moths, beetles, and mites land on sloths' back and nestle there, too. This is the world of the rainforest.

Listen, listen, and listen again. A jaguar cub cries out in pain. One million vicious army ants have attacked it. The cub cries out again, almost a death cry. Hercules beetles the size of oranges tap the ground near you with their pinchers. A great flock of scarlet macaws with wings three feet wide take off. You can hear the whirr. Toucan birds with huge bills pluck passion fruit with their five-inch bills. The sound is curious, one that you have never heard before. Tiny marsupial frogs jump almost silently off their mother's backs like little acrobats. You could hold one in your hand if they accidentally jumped down, but they jump along a tree branch nearby. This is the world of the rainforest.

Life hums in the rainforest understory above you and higher in the canopy. Beside you on the forest floor you can hear the hiss of snakes, the scamper of mice, the sucking sounds of an anteater. Rotting leaves on the floor of the forest make your stomach uneasy. Take a deeper breath, and you will smell perfumed flowers. This is the world of the rainforest.

When you open your eyes, you will have returned to a place you know, but remember the world where we have been, the world of a tropical rainforest.

The Bat: Script Based on a Mayan Creation Myth

I found a short version of this Mayan creation myth about fifteen years ago when I taught a children's theatre class that focused on stories from Latin America. I have told and retold the basic story many ways but prefer the simplicity of this version because most children can read the lines easily. After one or more tellings, they can speak the lines without scripts or improvise on their own.

Provide children with basic props—a colored scarf to represent each bird or a simple mask. Provide birds with colored feathers with strings attached or feathers with sticky tape to attach to bat. When the bat loses the feathers, they may be easily plucked off at the appropriate place in the story.

If children read the parts, assign the narrator roles to two children. If an adult leader does the narration, just one person may do it. Add a little action as the story dictates, but keep this simple if children are holding onto scripts.

Some librarians may wish to change the name "God" to "Creator" or even "Papa Deos" in public library settings.

The Story: The Bat

Narrator I: When time was in the cradle, there was no uglier creature than Bat. Bat lived in caves and lurked in dark places. Bat looked like those dark, dismal places.

Narrator II: Bat did not have feathers like the birds of the trees. But Bat could fly. Bat could fly like the birds of the trees.

Narrator I: The birds of the trees had feathers of glorious colors. Red. Orange. Pink. Yellow. Green. Blue. Bright, glorious colors.

Macaw: Macaw had red feathers.

Bird of Paradise: Bird of Paradise had orange feathers.

Flamingo: Flamingo had pink feathers.

Toucan: Toucan had yellow feathers.

Parrot: Parrot had green feathers.

Kingfisher: Kingfisher had blue feathers.

Narrator II: Bat looked around and saw the birds with their feathers of bright and glorious colors. And Bat began to envy them.

Narrator I: Bat decided to fly up to heaven to ask God to give him feathers.

Narrator II: But Bat did not tell God he was jealous. Bat was too clever to say that. Instead he asked God to give him feathers. He simply said . . .

Bat: Please, God, give me feathers. I am cold.

God: I don't have any feathers left to give you. I have no more feathers.

Bat: But I am cold nonetheless.

God: Go back to the world. Ask the birds. If you ask politely, perhaps all the birds will give you one of their feathers.

Narrator I: Bat did that. He flew back to the world. Politely, in his sweetest voice, he asked all the birds to give him a feather.

Bat: (*Calling*) Birds, beautiful birds! I am cold. Would you each please give me but one of your glorious feathers?

Macaw: Here is one of my red feathers.

Bat: Thank you, Macaw.

Bird of Paradise: I give you one of my orange feathers.

Bat: Thank you, too, Bird of Paradise.

Flamingo: I will let you have one of my best pink feathers.

Bat: I thank you for that pink feather, Flamingo.

Toucan: I can spare this little yellow feather.

Bat: And I will treasure this yellow feather, Toucan.

Parrot: Here is a beautiful green feather of mine.

Bat: Oh thank you, Parrot. It is indeed very beautiful.

Kingfisher: This is the brightest blue feather on my back. For you!

Bat: For me? Thank you, Kingfisher. Thank you.

Narrator I: The bat, glorious in his coat of many glorious colors flew high. He flew up to the clouds. He flew through the colors. He touched the mountaintops with his beauty.

Narrator II: Bat was proud of himself. He made the sky itself more beautiful.

Narrator I: The Zapotec people say that the rainbow was then born from the echo of his flight.

All Birds: Ahhhh. Ooooooo. The Rainbow. The Rainbow. The Rainbooooooow!

Narrator II: Now Bat became proud and prouder. Too proud. Much too proud. He thought he was more magnificent than any bird in the sky. He began to boast.

Bat: I am the most beautiful of all the creatures. I am the most beautiful. I am the most . . .

Narrator I: He began to say ugly words to the birds.

Bat: Ma-caw. Ma-caw. Haw! Haw! Haw!
Par-rot! Par-rot! Rot! Rot! Rot!
Tou-can! Tou-can! You're not as fine as I am!

All Birds: Let's do something about Bat.

Macaw: We should tell God.

Bird of Paradise: Yes, we should.

Flamingo: Tell God.

Toucan: I will.

Parrot: I will.

Kingfisher: We all will. We will all fly up to heaven. We will tell God to make Bat give back our feathers.

Birds: *(Calling to God)*: God, do something. Do something about Bat! He mocks us! He makes fun of us! He must give us back our feathers!

God: Stop! Stop this disharmony. My world is not a peaceful place with all this fighting. I shall come up with a plan.

Narrator I: God put a deep sleep upon Bat.

Narrator II: Sleep. Sleep. Sleep deep.

Narrator I: God caused bat's feathers to become loose. The feathers were barely hanging on bat's back. Bat awakened. He took off in flight, and all of his feathers fell like rain to the earth.

(Narrators I and II pull the feathers from bat's back and throw them down on the floor.)

Bat: My feathers! My glorious feathers! Ohhhhhh!

Narrator II: Bat lost his beautiful coat. Some say he is still looking for them.

Narrator I: But Bat is ashamed to go out looking for his feathers during daylight. He only flies at night. To this day, he has not found his feathers.

Narrator II: Many say he is blind as a bat.

All Birds: Now you know the whole story. And this is the end of the tale.

The Finest Flying Frog in the Jungle

Read this story aloud or tell it to a group of elementary-age children. To add interest, make flannel board characters to place on the wall. For an even more interesting, interactive story, have children make large stick puppets or provide them with hand puppets of the different animal characters. As these animals appear in the story, children move the puppets when the flying frog figure jumps near them. With a large group, many children may make duplicates of the animals—harpy eagle, howler monkey, chameleon, anaconda snake. As the storyteller proceeds with the story, the whole room will then become a flurry of rainforest animals!

Please note that the terms "jungle" and "rainforest" are used interchangeably in this story for the sake of language resonance. Strictly speaking, a jungle is a dense area of growth found at the edges of the rainforest. Jungles also grow where trees have been cut, but if this area is left alone, it may become a rainforest.

The Story

Once there was a flying frog who lived in a rainforest. He was a young flying frog without much wisdom. And when one is young and inexperienced, he begins to think proud thoughts about himself. Young Flying Frog became so proud, so inflated with his own importance, that he believed he was the finest flying frog in the jungle!

Flying Frog had not traveled far. He lived in the top of one tree in the rainforest, and had not even seen the rest of the rainforest. He thought that all of the rainforest must be exactly like the top of his own tree. As he grew, frog began to make small leaps into nearby treetops.

One day he decided to take a longer journey, a journey to the rest of the rainforest. He wanted to tell the other creatures, "I am the finest flying frog in the jungle. I am the most aerodynamic. I am the most musical. I am the most colorful. And I am the most daring animal in the rainforest!"

So Flying Frog took off. He glided from branch to branch. Flaps of skin on his strong little legs helped him glide over to a faraway tree. He had never gone so far. Flying Frog felt fantastic. He called out in his loudest voice, "I am the finest flying frog in the jungle. I am the most aerodynamic. I am the most musical. I am the most colorful. And I am the most daring animal in the rainforest."

Whoosh! Just then above Flying Frog's head soared Harpy Eagle. Harpy Eagle was three feet long, almost ten times bigger than Flying Frog. Harpy Eagle had claws, claws as big as the hands of people who lived in the rainforest. Harpy Eagle flew fast, almost as fast as an automobile on the highway.

Harpy Eagle was the most aerodynamic animal Flying Frog could ever imagine. He said, "Oh my! Eagle can certainly fly! I can't fly that fast. Well, at least I am the finest flying *frog* in the jungle. I may not be the most aerodynamic, but I am the most musical. I am the most colorful. And I am the most daring animal in the rainforest."

Flying Frog took off again. This time he used his little webfeet and the flaps of skin on his legs to parachute down. Down, down went Flying Frog, beneath the forest emergent layer. Down to the rich green canopy. Many animals Flying Frog had never seen lived there.

Yow! Yow! Yow! Hoooowwwwwl!" howled Howler Monkey. Howler Monkey and his seven friends hooted and howled together.

Their voices were so amazingly loud that Flying Frog knew that his croak was no match for the howls of Howler Monkey. He said, "Oh my! Howler Monkey's cry sounds like a whole rainforest rock concert! Well, at least I'm the finest flying frog in the jungle. I may not be the most musical, but I am the most colorful. And I am the most daring animal in the rainforest."

Flying Frog took off once again. He parachuted down, down below the canopy. Down to the dark understory of the rainforest, he went. Flying Frog couldn't see very well. Sunlight became dimmer in the understory layer. And, although he couldn't see well, Flying Frog still thought he must be the most colorful animal in the rainforest.

Just then a quick-moving creature turned black, then brown, then yellow, then orange, then green, and then brown again. Flying Frog could not believe his eyes. In less than a minute, Chameleon looked like a streak of the rainbow spreading through the rainforest.

Flying Frog said, "Oh my! Chameleon's a sight for sore eyes. Well, at least I'm the finest flying frog in the jungle. I may not be the most colorful. But I am the most daring animal in the rainforest."

Flying Frog was getting tired, but once again he used his strong legs to parachute down, down below the understory. He reached the rainforest floor. It was so dark, Flying Frog could hardly see his own webby toes. He tippy-toed over to the edge of the river. There in the shadows of the forest floor, Flying Frog saw Anaconda Snake.

Anaconda Snake was big. Anaconda Snake was ten times bigger than Harpy Eagle. Anaconda Snake slithered over to the river and wrapped its fat body around Jaguar and suffocated the cat's muscular body.

Flying Frog froze. Then Flying Frog trembled. Flying Frog was too frightened to make a sound. He knew then that he was *not* the most daring animal in the rainforest.

On his webby, webby toes, Flying Frog made his way from the rainforest floor up to the shadowy understory. He worked very hard to go up to the canopy. And with his greatest effort he returned to the emergent treetops of the rainforest.

"Oh my," he said. "A flying frog is not the finest animal in the rainforest. Harpy Eagle is the most aerodynamic. Howler Monkey is the most musical. Chameleon is the most colorful. And Anaconda Snake is the most daring. But I can fly and I can sing. I am a beautiful green color with brilliant red-orange eyes. And I did go on a very long, daring adventure. I don't know all the flying frogs in the jungle. But, I am a very fine flying frog in this very fine rainforest. I should know because I've been there!"

So it was on this day that Flying Frog became not so young, not so inexperienced, and not so boastful. Flying Frog had become something else much more important. He had become wise.

Rainforest Action Sheet

How You Can Help Save Rainforests

Capitalize on kids' good intentions to do what they can to save rainforests and our environment in general. Launch a letter-writing campaign to government officials and business organizations about specific issues. Letter-writing campaigns to companies have made big strides in changing destructive practices such as cutting down rainforests. Recently environmental efforts have not been as well supported as they were in the past.

Join local environmental awareness groups to find out what to do your local community. Search Web sites of the WWF (World Wildlife Federation/World Wide Fund for Nature; www.wwf.org) and the children's link of the Rainforest Action Network (www.ran.org/kids_action). These Web sites include many specific things kids can do.

Instead of rewarding children for books read during one month of a summer reading program, give money the library would ordinarily spend on prizes to a local zoo or global fund raising program. Chart the course of kids' reading as a whole. For example "Kids at the Southside Branch Read 1,000 books during the first week in June. Because of this, the Library will contribute $250 to save rainforests!" Since children become accustomed to taking some tangible thing home, give away free posters and rainforest activity sheets. On each activity sheet, remind kids that their reading has been helping save the rainforests.

Art for "A Glimpse of Tropical Rainforests"

Rainforest Masks

Photocopy the three masks of the monkey, jaguar, and tree frog for each child. Provide markers or colored pencils to decorate the masks. Instruct children to cut out the masks along the solid dark lines. The masks may be attached to dowels to hold up to the face, or holes may be punched at the sides and elastic cord inserted to make facemasks. If these are used as facemasks, holes should be cut for eye openings.

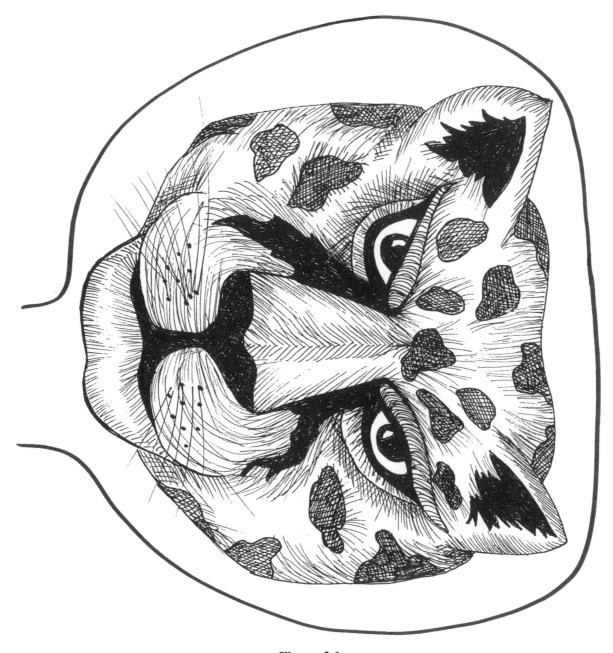

Figure 2.1

Figure 2.2

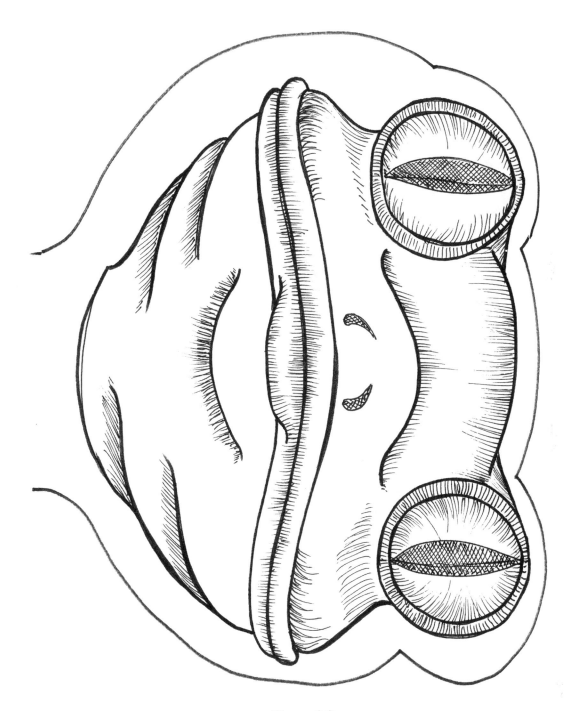

Figure 2.3

Puppets or Props for the Story "The Bat"

Photocopy the drawings of the birds and the bat and provide children with colored markers to decorate them. Instruct children to cut these out, leaving a little white space around the edges. Tape craft sticks to the backs of these figures for children to move as the teacher reads the story "The Bat." For a more dramatic presentation, enlarge these figures or have children draw their own large animals on poster boards as they reenact the story read by a librarian or storyteller.

Figure 2.4. Bat

Figure 2.5. Macaw

Figure 2.6. Toucan

Figure 2.7. Kingfisher

Figure 2.8. Parrot

Figure 2.9. Bird of Paradise

Figure 2.10. Flamingo

Puppets for the Story "The Finest Flying Frog"

Photocopy the five animals—Flying Frog, Harpy Eagle, Chameleon, Howler Monkey, Anaconda Snake—for stick puppets to retell the story "The Finest Flying Frog." Children may want to draw these animals on a larger scale, or the teacher may want to make felt flannel board figures to tell the story as a flannel board story.

Figure 2.11. Harpy Eagle

Figure 2.12. Flying Frog

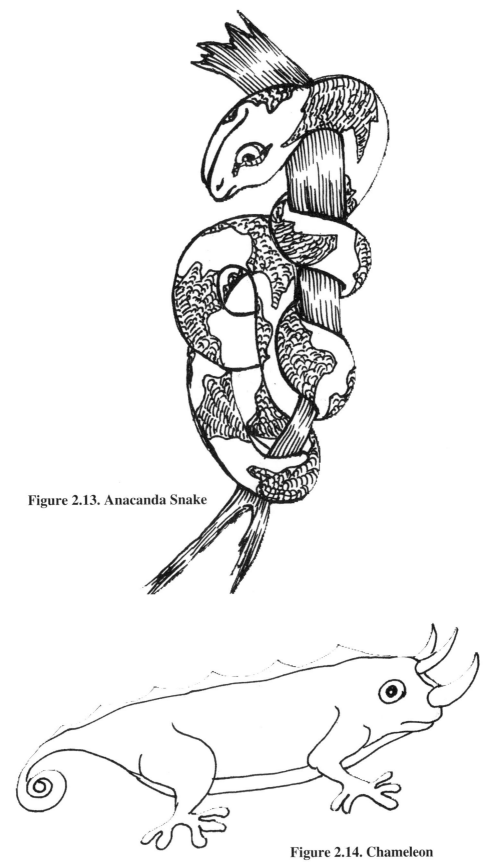

Figure 2.13. Anacanda Snake

Figure 2.14. Chameleon

Figure 2.15. Howler Monkey

3

Animals Down Under

Can you imagine an animal that is part duck and part mammal? It looks so weird that the first time you see it, you think it's fake! Is there an animal that can jump but not walk or run? Have you heard of a bird that doesn't fly and a possum that does? Is this a chapter on science fiction, or is it a chapter on the isolated but very real continent-island of Australia? If you guess that the strange animals described in the beginning of this paragraph actually exist in the outback of Australia, you are correct and probably curious to read more about these creatures of the faraway island continent.

Australia, the isolated continent in the Southern Hemisphere of our earth, seems somehow unrelated to all the other places we could visit. According to scientists, it was part of a larger landmass, a kind of super continent that also contained South America, Asia, Africa, and Antarctica. It separated from the other continents and has been isolated for 50 million years. Thus, the plants and animals found here were left to evolve in a way of their own. Because of this, we find animals that cannot be found anywhere else on earth. This uniqueness fascinates children who love the study of animals especially the study of wild animals.

Australia is a wild land, an unspoiled wilderness with exotic wildlife. Travel guides agree that the amazing fauna is one of the country's biggest attractions. Although Australia does have domesticated animals introduced from the Western world, these are not covered here. The birds and mammals unique to Australia are the main focus. They are so unusual that many cannot be found in smaller zoos in the United States. Through videos and films we can experience the span of a kangaroo's jump, the waddle of a wombat, and the scary sight of a frilled lizard in action. Through reading the myths and legends of this land and looking at the brightly colored aboriginal paintings, we can gain further insight into the wonders of Australian animals.

This chapter explores orders of animals that are peculiar to Australia—marsupials (mammals with pockets) and monotremes (mammals that lay eggs). Although one kind of marsupial, the possum, is found in the United States, none of the other more exotic varieties can be seen outside of zoos or exotic animal farms. Australia's birds are a birdwatcher's paradise. From the smaller birds that fly to the big birds that do not, we encounter the beautifully feathered lyrebird as well as the huge emu. Brightly colored parrots and fancy cockatoos fill trees, and kookaburras entertain humans by imitating the sounds of other birds.

By studying these special animals, children enlarge their minds for discovery of knowledge beyond the environments in which they live. As kids learn about the habits and behavior of these animals, they can develop skills necessary for sound science study. Those skills include observing, classifying, inferring, and hypothesizing. Many of the same skills apply in other content areas found throughout the curriculum. For example, careful observation is valuable in writing in all fields of study. Students of history and science need to observe details when they read and to classify information into categories of things that are alike and things that are different from one another. They then need to draw inferences to come up with premises and hypotheses.

The project and programs found here will inspire student research, writing, dramatic play, and art projects as well as introducing geographic and literary topics. Vocabularies will grow as students encounter the terms "outback," "down under," "indigenous," and "aboriginal" as well as the names of Australian animals and animal orders. In a larger context, understanding Australian animal life will open children's minds to an unusual mind-set, that of "dreamtime." A deep understanding of dreamtime will be difficult for most of us to conceive, but on some level we can describe this thinking so that children will begin to see aboriginal Australian story and beliefs different from their own. Paul Morin's book *Animal Dreaming* (listed in the bibliography) will help children understand this concept on a basic level.

Nonfiction, fiction, and picture books are listed in the bibliography along with story collections and project books. Picture books and fiction have been limited to more realistic titles rather than more whimsical books by noted author Mem Fox. While Fox's books are delightful and recommended for reading aloud to younger students, this chapter focuses on the informational nature of the topic. Most of us will probably not take a trip to Australia, but the programs and ideas described here can help children visualize a trek across the outback through reading books from the bibliography and engaging in the program activities suggested next.

Bibliography

Arnold, Caroline. *Australian Animals*. HarperCollins, 2000.

One-page summaries of various animals with colored photographs will give students a basic overall understanding of the varieties living in Australia. The animals are organized by the different habitats—forests, grasslands, deserts, and water's edge.

Carmi, Rebecca. *Expedition Down Under*. Scholastic, 2001.

This Magic School Bus chapter book tells about Ms. Frizzle's trip to Australia with her students. While the story reads as a fictional narrative, readers will learn much about such Australian animals as the dingo, kangaroo, and spiny anteater. The information appears as short student reports set in an appealing notebook-page format.

Cobb, Vicki. *This Place Is Lonely*. Illustrated by Barbara Lavallee. Walker and Company, 1991.

Australian animals are briefly described and illustrated in this picture book on Australia. The emu and cassowary, two large and unusual birds, are shown as well as the marsupials native to Australia. The style of illustration is especially noteworthy because it captures the design of aboriginal art.

Coxon, Michele. *Too Big!* Star Bright Books, 2000.

Sparse text and lift-the-flap illustrations tell the story of a young wallaby who wants to stay in his mother's pouch. In looking for another place to rest, the wallaby discovers the pouch, nest, or dwelling places of numerous other Australian animals. Although this picture book may be used for very young children, the basic information and illustrations are useful for primary elementary grades as well.

Eugene, Toni. *Koalas and Kangaroos: Strange Animals of Australia*. Books for Young Explorers, National Geographic Society, 1981.

Easy text and bright photos will appeal to primary grades and introduce Australian marsupials from spiny anteaters and bandicoots to kangaroos and wallabies as well as birds from emus to kookaburras. Other unusual animals such as the frilled lizard and goanna add interest. Details in text supply special information such as the fact that bowerbirds love blue so much, they might even collect blue clothespins to decorate their nests and that loannas stand as tall as children!

Fenton, Julie. *Kangaroos and Other Marsupials*. Blackbirch Press, 1997.

One of World Book's series of Animals of the World, this volume is structured around twenty-five questions that cover unusual topics such as "Do Tasmanian Devils Throw Tantrums?" and "Where Do Koalas Hang Out?"

Franklin, Sharon, Rhonda Krafchin, and Cynthia Black. *Artisans around the World, Southwest Pacific*. Raintree Steck-Vaughn, 2000.

This volume of an outstanding multicultural arts series is devoted to the arts of Australia, New Guinea, New Zealand, and Indonesia. The project for Australia is an excellent x-ray painting example that older elementary children will enjoy.

Leach, Michael. *Koala*. Raintree Steck-Vaughn, 2003.

Part of the Natural World Series, this volume introduces the koala's birth, survival techniques, and unusual behavior including sleeping about eighteen hours a day. Outstanding photographs detail the koala's life cycle.

McLeod, Pauline E., Francis Firebrace Jones, and June E. Barker. *Gadi Mirrabooka: Australian Aboriginal Tales from the Dreaming*. Libraries Unlimited, 2001.

Thirty-three aboriginal tales from Australia include many about animals. A long introduction discusses history, customs, the people, and geography of the continent. An excellent resource for reading aloud and for storytellers to adapt in the retelling.

Miller-Schroeder, Patricia. *Kangaroos*. Raintree Steck-Vaughn, 2002.

Part of the Untamed World series, this detailed text provides information for middle to upper elementary grades about kangaroo characteristics, food, habitats, social behavior, and folklore traditions. According to Aboriginal legends, the first kangaroos came to live in Australia through huge windstorms that blew these creatures through the air, and in struggling to reach the ground, the kangaroo's back legs grew long and strong enough for them to hop.

Morgan, Sally. *The Flying Emu and Other Australian Stories*. Knopf, 1992.

This rich collection of Australian legends includes twenty stories with brightly colored stylized illustrations that reflect the folk-art tradition of the text. Some stories center on the early people of this land, and others focus on such animals as the emu, crocodile, kangaroo, and kookabura.

Morin, Paul. *Animal Dreaming*. Silver Whistle, Harcourt Brace & Company, 1998.

In this original story, a young Aboriginal boy is taught important lessons about the beginning of Dreamtime and creation from an elder. In the storytelling, the boy learns that the kangaroo, turtle, and emu bring about peace when other animals are fighting. The fighting animals turn into parts of the landscape. Crocodile becomes stone, snakes make hills, and fish become large water holes.

Oodgeroo. *Dreamtime, Aboriginal Stories*. Illustrated by Bronwyn Bancroft. Lothrop, Lee & Shepard, 1994.

The stories were retold along with stories from her childhood by a much-loved Australian storyteller who worked as an author and artist. An aboriginal artist has illustrated the stories in this volume and will inspire children to try their own examples of this style of art.

Paul, Tessa. *Down Under*. Crabtree, 1998.

Part of the Animal Trackers Around the World series, this slender volume is densely packed with information about eleven Australian animals. Unique physical features, habits and behavior, drawings, and sample footprints are included for each animal.

Penny, Malcolm. *The Secret World of Kangaroos*. Raintree Steck-Vaughn, 2002.

Detailed information about kangaroo behavior, reproduction, and social behavior in this volume complements the information in the Miller-Schroeder volume. In addition to the large red and grey kangaroos, smaller members of this family include the wallabies and tree kangaroos, which are also described and photographed. Kangaroo fighting patterns as well as development of joeys are shown in clear photographs.

Sayre, April Pulley. *G'Day, Australia*. Millbrook Press, 2003.

Basic text and lively photographs introduce Australia and its many unusual animals. Australia's various biomes including deserts and savannas called "the brush" are explained.

Short, Joan, Jack Green, and Bettina Bird. *Platypus*. Illustrated by Andrew Wichlinski. Mondo, 1996.

Describes physical characteristics and behavior of this fascinating freshwater animal that lives only in Australia. With an odd combination of webbed feet, duckbill, and fur, the platypus feeds in water, breathes air with nostrils above the water, lays eggs, and, like mammals, feeds its young with milk.

Spurling, Margaret. *Bilby Moon*. Illustrated by Danny Snell. Kane/Miller, 2001.

In this gentle tale, a little bilby who is fascinated by the moon becomes concerned when the full moon begins to disappear. She asks other Australian animals to help her find it, only to be reassured by Owl that the moon appears and disappears as a matter of course.

Stodart, Eleanor. *The Australian Echidna*. Houghton Mifflin, 1991.

Physical characteristics, development and behavior of this spiny anteater are described through text and colored photographs. Like the platypus, this egg-laying mammal, was only discovered about two hundred years ago by European naturalists and given its own class of monotremes. Detailed photographs show the spines and the holes left by burrowing echidnas as they hide from predators.

Tesar, Jenny. *What on Earth Is a Quokka?* Blackbirch Press, 1997.

The text discusses characteristics and behavior of this marsupial, native to Australia. The more common name for this animal, is the wallaby. It is much smaller than a kangaroo and was first thought to be a giant rat.

Vaughan, Marcia. *Snap!* Illustrated by Sascha Hutchinson. Scholastic, 1996.

Joey kangaroo learns many games when he pesters various animals to play with him. But Joey's persistence proves dangerous when he asks a crocodile to play. This is a good story for reading aloud that is accompanied by clever torn-paper collage illustrations.

Vaughan, Marcia. *Wombat Stew*. Illustrated by Pamela Lofts. Silver Burdett, 1986.

A series of Australian animals give Dingo many gooey, chewy ideas for his wombat stew. Just when Dingo is ready to add a wombat to his stew, all the animals remind him to taste the broth first. Dingo discovers they have tricked him, but the damage has been done. Poisoned by the brew, Dingo retreats forever.

Weigelt, Udo. *The Wild Wombat*. Illustrated by Anne-Katrin Piepenbrink. Translated by Kathryn Grell. North-South, 2002.

Originally published in German, this fascinating picture book recounts the tale of zoo animals who overreact when they hear a wild wombat will be coming to the zoo. The reader will peek under the split pages of the book to see what scary creature each animal imagines the wombat to resemble. In the end, the wombat shows them his tame appearance and teaches them to not jump to conclusions in the future.

Trekking after Australian Animals: A School Program

This program gives students opportunities to research and write about Australian animals. The games and activities planned for a school media center can also be used in classroom settings. The teacher/media specialist can prepare the games, or students may create them individually or in small groups. The student diary project may involve art lessons or a study of aboriginal art. The map project involves research and visual display skills. The storytelling portion may take one class period or several if students wish to write their own stories from the scenarios provided in this chapter. Students will practice oral language skills and dramatic expression in this activity.

Materials Needed

1. Box of business-sized envelopes

2. Pack of one hundred 3 x 5–inch index cards

3. Pack of 4 x 6–inch index cards for Aussie Animal Concentration game

4. Several poster boards

Procedures

1. Create a set of envelopes and cards to play the Aussie Animal Mystery Game. Write the situation or question on the outside of a standard 3½ x 6½–inch business envelope and provide a blank index card 3 x 5 inches for students to write their answers and insert inside the envelope.

   Each card describes a situation that a student traveler might encounter on a trip to Australia. The media specialist will want to make a few sample envelopes for students to guide them in making their own game envelopes. This activity will test students' research skills and provide other students with an entertaining learning experience. See the boxed examples that follow.

2. Make a set of "Aussie Animal Concentration" cards for a simple game of concentration.

3. Have students make their own Australian animal diaries. Provide them with notebooks and pencils. For a "bark-like" Australian art touch, cover the notebooks with crumbled brown paper with aboriginal art designs. Guidelines for a diary are provided in this chapter.

4. Suggest one of the following alternative projects to the diary for students with geographic and artistic interests. These projects include making a map or doing art in an aboriginal Australian style. These projects are described in this chapter.

5. Do storytelling and scriptwriting projects with your students. Simply retelling the book *Wombat Stew* by having students chant the wombat stew song is the easiest project. For more involved activities, use the story scenarios and guidelines for script writing that appear at the end of this section.

The Aussie Animal Mystery Game

Create a set of "situation envelopes" with blank index cards to insert in each envelope to play this game. On the outside of a standard 3½ inch x 6½–inch business envelope, write out a situation a student might encounter on an Australian trip. Then insert a 3 x 5–inch index card inside each envelope for students to write their responses.

Teachers may want to create all the situations or give students a few samples for them to write their own game envelopes. Here are a few examples to use as models.

Situation One:	**Situation Two:**	**Situation Three:**
You are walking in a forested area of Australia. The air smells like cough drops. In the branches of a nearby tree, you see a cute little animal. Is it safe to pet? What is it? Why do the air and the animal smell like cough drops?	On a walkabout you see something that looks like a small dragon. Suddenly the dragon leaps to the ground as it catches a little rat-like creature. Who are the animals and is the dragon poisonous?	You are walking in a desert in Australia. Out of the corner of your eye, you see an animal waddling along. You turn to move in its direction, but, the animal has disappeared. What was it? And what is that spiny looking thing left in the sand?

Aussie Animal Concentration

Make a set of cards to play this game. On one side of the card, draw a picture of an Australian animal or use a photograph from a Web site to print a picture of the animal. The following site gives facts and colored pictures for about twenty-five animals: www.giveusahome.co.uk/australian/animals.htm. On the reverse side of the card, provide the name of the animal and three facts.

Students can play the game several ways. For a simple concentration game, place five or six cards on the table. Ask children to identify the animals if they can. Remove the cards. Now ask students to remember what animal cards were shown on the table and give the names.

To make the game more challenging, let students study the cards until they can remember something about the animals. Shuffle the cards and place them face side up on the table. You may want to start with only ten or twelve cards. Ask students to name each animal and give at least one fact about it.

Guidelines for a Sample Australian Animal Diary

You have just been given a study grant to learn about Australian animals. You will be concentrating on animal life in the outback areas of this continent. You have packed a sketchbook and colored pencils, but you have forgotten your camera. In your sketchbook, draw pictures of ten animals and describe them in a detailed narrative account. This diary will be shared with fellow students when you return from your trip.

Australian Animal Map

The map is an alternative to the diary. Provide a large map of Australia to students or have them make their own outline on a large poster board. Ask students to research where various Australian animals live and place pictures of those animals in the appropriate places on the map. The pictures may be drawn or copied from the Internet sources listed in this chapter.

Aboriginal Art Animals Adapted

Using the patterns provided (Figure 3.1) and the illustration, invite students to design in the manner of an aboriginal illustration. Originally, aboriginal artists did their designs on tree bark, but today they use paper. You can reproduce the designs on tan paper for this more authentic touch.

Show students the techniques of cross-hatching, dots, and wavy lines to use in their work. This art is very sophisticated, but simply using these techniques will give children an idea of stylized Australian art. Note that two illustrations are given for each animal. Older students will want to fill in the blank outlines of the animals. Younger students may be given the fully designed animal to color with colored pencils or markers.

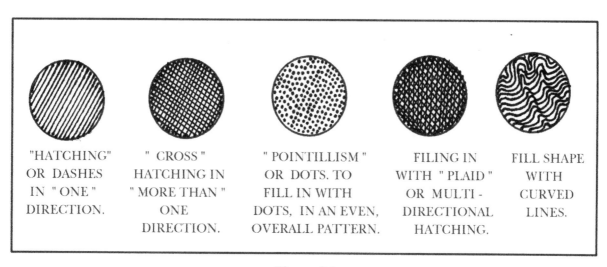

Figure 3.1

Figure 3.2. Kangaroo

Figure 3.3. Kangaroo

Figure 3.4. Platypus

Figure 3.5. Platypus

Figure 3.6. Lizard

Figure 3.7. Lizard

Storytelling and Script Writing

When Emus Could Fly

Story Scenario: Once Emus had beautiful rainbow-colored feathers and they could fly. But the one particular Emu caused all of this to change. Emu became too proud of himself and expected all animals to bow to his every wish. He ordered Frog to get out of his way. He poked fun at Kangaroo's tail. He told Kookabura he had an ugly laugh. So Kookaburra decided to teach him a lesson.

Kookaburra challenged Emu to a race. The race would be a race to the sun. To convince Emu to take part in such a long journey, Kookaburra began flattering the vain bird. Every day for three days Kookabura flattered Emu. The last compliment became so excessive that Emu felt he must participate in the race or he would be the laughing stock of the country.

The race was set with all animals in attendance. Kangaroo was in charge, so he declared that Emu must go first because he was larger than Kookabura. Frog gave the opening call. Emu took off, leaving Kookabura sitting in a safe tree far away.

As Emu got closer to the sun, all the animals back on ground and in the trees saw a ball of fire near the sun. The fireball came closer to Earth until it landed in a billabong, the stagnant pool of water nearby.

When the fire burned out, the animals saw a very different Emu in front of them. Emu's feathers were no longer beautiful and long, but had burned down to small stubbly feathers the color of mud. Emu was so embarrassed, he began to run and didn't stop running for days upon days. When Emu finally stopped, his legs had become strong—a fast runner indeed. Had he learned his lesson? No, not really. Emu still is too proud of himself. But all he can boast about are his strong legs.

Note: Turn the story scenario into a script following these guidelines:

1. Have a narrator set the scene. For example, the narrator might read the first three lines of the story scenario.

2. Create specific dialogue for the various animals. For example, instead of the line "He ordered Frog to get out of his way," have Emu say, "Frog, get out of my way!" Then have Frog either hop to one side or say "Right-o!"

3. Proceed with interspersing narration with dialogue as you continue to tell the story. Make up extra dialogue to keep the story lively.

4. Add actions as side notes along with the lines.

5. Give the script a good closure. The narrator might give a moral, or the main character could speak directly to the audience. For example, the Emu could say, "I may not have beautiful feathers, but look at my wonderful strong legs! I am very proud of my legs. I have the best legs in the whole world!"

Four Other Stories to Adapt

Four other stories that can be successfully adapted for creative dramatics activities may be found in the book *Gadi Mirrabooka: Australian Aboriginal Tales from the Dreaming* retold by Pauline McLeod, Francis Firebrace Jones, and June Baker (Libraries Unlimited, 2001).

I recommend using "Why the Kookaburra Laughs," "First Platypus, Gaygar—The Little Mother Duck," "How the Kangaroo Got Her Pouch," and "How Koolah the Koala Lost His Tail."

Give the narrative lines to several narrators and the dialogue to different children, or create more dialogue instead of using excessive narrative to create a lively script.

Animals Down Under:
A Public Library Program

This program may be scheduled for one to two hours depending on how many activities the librarian chooses to use. Several games, craft projects, and stories have been developed in this section. Begin with a story while students are alert, then proceed to a craft or quiet activity and end with more active games, because children tend to become restless after awhile. Wind-down time may be advised rather than actually ending on a high-pitched note. A final activity with participation, such as reading aloud a story in which everyone takes part, works well.

Materials Needed

1. Package of 4 x 6–inch index cards

2. Photocopies of animal masks and heavy paper (Figures 3.8–3.10)

3. Elastic cording (12 inches per child)

4. Multiple pairs of scissors

5. Fine-tip markers, medium-tip markers, assorted colored pencils

6. Feathers, construction paper scraps for masks

Procedures

1. Begin with a creative dramatics project of Australian animal acrobatics. Encourage children to move like Australian animals. For example, "Curl up in a ball and burrow like an echidna." "Balance yourself on your back tail then jump like a kangaroo." "Glide into water like a playpus." "Show your frills like a frilled lizard, then run away on your back legs."

2. Play the Kangaroo Relay Game.

3. Play a new version of musical chairs with the Australian Animal Walkabout Game. See directions in this chapter.

4. Have children make animal masks. Use the patterns provided in this chapter if you wish, and have plenty of other materials to decorate the masks. Markers, construction paper scraps, and feathers add decorative touches.

5. End the program by reading a story such as Paul Morrin's *Animal Dreaming* or *Snap!* by Marcia Vaughan.

Kangaroo Relay Game

You will need two aprons with pockets (such as a chef's or baker's apron) and two kangaroo puppets or stuffed animals for this game. Follow these directions for playing the game.

Divide group into two relay teams that will race each other. Line up the teams at one end of the room, and place a kangaroo puppet or stuffed animal at the opposite end of the room, one for each team. The first child in each line is designated "Kangaroo Mama," and the leader ties an apron with a front pocket on each child. At the beginning signal, the Kangaroo Mamas jump across the room to pick up the baby Joeys who have hopped away from the pouch. Mamas place Joeys in their pouches and hop back to the line. They hand the Joey to the second child and tie the Mama aprons on the third child in each line.

The second child holding Joey crouches down and hops the puppet to the opposite side of the room again, as if Joey were hopping away. The second child hops back to the line where the third child (a new Kangaroo Mama) repeats the action of the first Kangaroo Mama. Play continues in this fashion until all children have hopped or one team finishes first.

Australian Animal Walkabout

This variation of musical chairs adds children to the game rather than eliminating them. Tell children they will be doing an Australian Animal Walkabout. Because some of these creatures have been endangered in the past, we will not want to eliminate them. Instead, everyone will remain in the play at the end of the game. In preparation, tape an index card to the under side of each chair. On the index card, write the name of an Australian animal with an action appropriate for that animal to do. Follow the directions that follow.

Instructions for Australian Animal Walkabout.

Begin play by humming "The Animals Go Walking All About" to the tune of "The Ants Go Marching" as children walk around the room in a circle. The leader marches with children. At the end of the first stanza, the leader points to a child and tells him or her to sit down on a chair that has been placed in the middle of the room. The humming continues as children walk about and another child sits down on a second chair that the leader adds to the middle. Humming and walking continues until all children are seated in chairs.

When everyone is seated, instruct children to look at the card taped to his or her chair. One by one each child does the action so that the group may guess which animals have participated in the walkabout.

Featured animals may include wombat, dingo, platypus, echindna, emu, kangaroo, kookabura, and other birds and reptiles found in Australia. You may need to repeat animal roles if your group of children is large.

Art for "Animals Down Under"

Animal Masks

Photocopy the three animal masks on heavy paper and supply children with markers and colored pencils to decorate them. Instruct kids to cut out the masks along the heavy black lines.

To prepare these as facemasks, cut out the eye sections, and punch holes where indicated. Tie ribbons in the holes or attach a twelve-inch length of elastic cording through the holes.

Aboriginal Australian Art

Traditional Australian aboriginal art is a very stylized form of decoration. Show children examples of this art found in pictures of books listed in this chapter's bibliography. Give them the solid outlines of kangaroo, platypus, and lizard to decorate. Display the little chart with examples of typical decoration (hatching, pointillism, and curved lines) to choose from.

Younger students may be content to simply color in the already-decorated figures, but older children and budding artists will like learning this style of design for themselves. Examples of both projects are shown in this chapter.

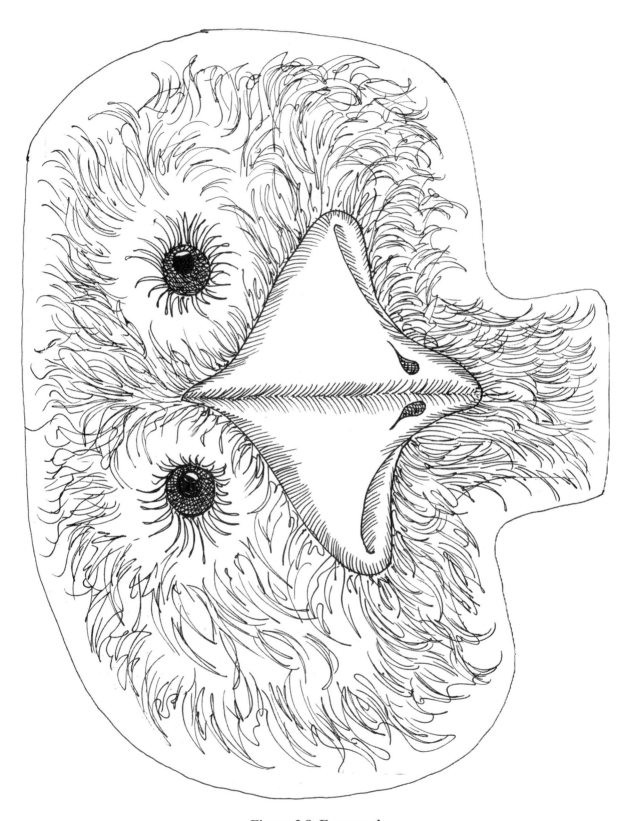

Figure 3.8. Emu mask

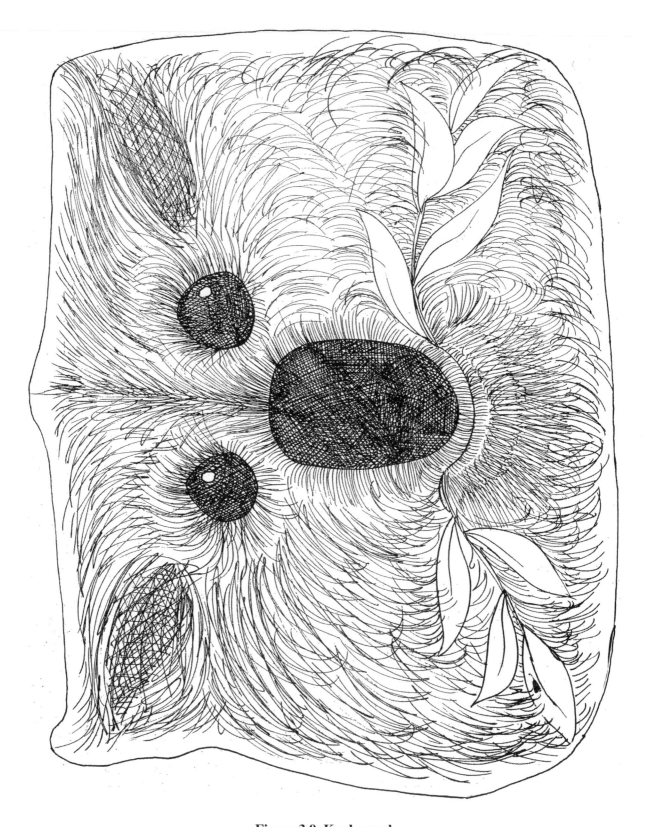

Figure 3.9. Koala mask

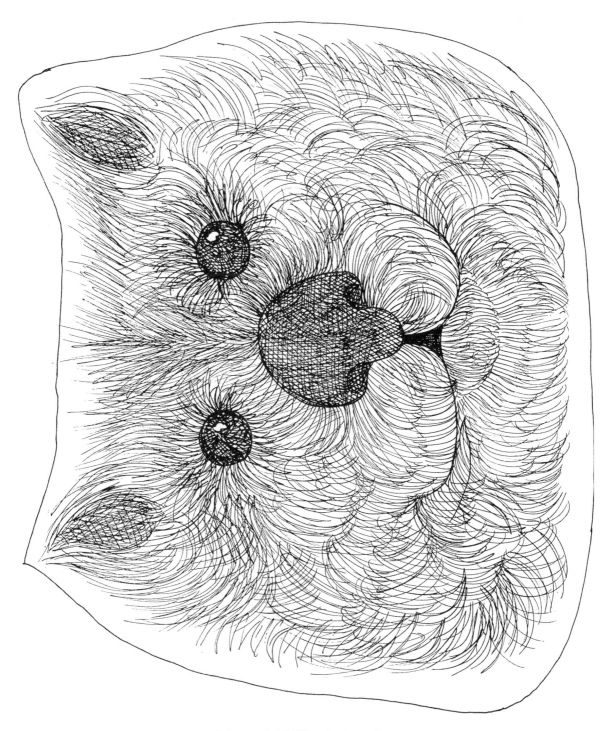

Figure 3.10. Wombat mask

Egyptian Mythology:
A Glimpse into Eternity

Just when we think children have become blasé about our world and its sophisticated technologies, we can still capture their interest with stories of ancient Egyptian gods and mysteries that reach back over five thousand years ago. Why is this? What value does the study of ancient mythology have for children today? How does mythology relate to the information scientists provide us?

Many children are totally fascinated about ancient Egypt beyond school assignments. In my experience in public libraries, there never seem to be enough books available on this topic. Elementary schools routinely include units on Egypt in the upper grades, but children seek out information for themselves long before and after school assignments.

From the time we begin telling stories to children, we naturally engage young minds in tales of adventure. The old stories that explain how the rainbow came to be or why stars appear in the sky or what are we doing on this earth continue to be told and retold for all generations. Stories about how things came to be are called myths. Myths make sense of our universe.

Students who study mythology learn to observe the natural world and relate that world to their own lives. In prescientific days, people lived in fear of the elements and of phenomena they could not explain. Creating stories and giving a structure to those stories gave early people a way to gain some psychological control over their world. As children learn about these stages in the story of human existence, they gain meaning and internalize the process for themselves. Science gives us facts and theories. It may tell us how things happened. The worlds of myth, literature, and poetry open our minds to another dimension. They help us think about the possible "whys."

Although children are naturally fascinated about Egyptian mythology, as they research the stories, they will face contradictions and become confused. Contradictory stories do exist about creation of the gods. Remember, the Egyptian civilization was a lengthy one. Beliefs changed over the course of time, but change took place slowly, often reluctantly. Old beliefs did not necessarily give way to the new ones. Old cosmologies (belief systems) continued right along with new ideas. Local gods from one region were added to other gods from another region. After thousands of years, the sun god Ra might be known as Atun-Ra or Amun-Ra. Also, a god or goddess did not stay in a certain locality or become associated with only one animal or characteristic as in ancient Greece or Rome, nor did Egyptian gods inhabit the same world with humans as they did in these other ancient cultures. Although the pharaoh was a human king, the Egyptian people had little contact with the actual pharaoh. This was their god on earth; only a small number of people ever saw him and only in an annual, highly formalized ritual setting.

This chapter summarizes some of the ancient beliefs and myths for the teacher and librarian as they guide student research. The bibliography directs students to a variety of sources about the mythology and includes collections of myths. Useful Web sites to order materials include www.kingtutshop.com and www.legendarytoys.com.

The program guides in this chapter summarize some myths that children can retell on their own. These give opportunities for student writing and storytelling. The full-length script "Great Sun, Great River" can be used in both school and public library settings. The public library program looks at this topic in a less "report"-oriented way and focuses on reading a story or retelling a legend then giving children an opportunity to make one or more of the three craft projects described.

Notes about Basic Egyptian Beliefs

Because the basic chronology of the creation of gods in ancient Egypt is not straightforward, I summarize here some of the ideas to guide the educator. The Egyptian kingdom lasted thousands of years. Recorded history traces this early civilization from about 4500 B.C., although the land was divided between two distinct groups of people. One civilization lived south from Aswan to Memphis. Memphis is about fifteen miles south of present-day Cairo. This was called Upper Egypt because the Nile River seemed to stretch upward. Lower Egypt was located north of Memphis. These two regions became united about 3500 B.C.

The cosmologies were even more divided. At least four systems have been identified. People in the Memphis area believed the god Ptah created the god Atum, as well as the other gods, just by saying their names. Ptah was so sacred, he created a whole group of gods known as the Ennead. The Ennead consisted of Atum (Sun), Shu (Air), Tefnut (Rain), Nut (Sky), Geb (Earth). From Geb and Nut came Osiris, Isis, Seth, and Nephthys. Some sources say Geb and Nut made the other four gods, but other sources seem to gloss over this idea and simply say that Ptah made them all.

Other regions developed different belief systems. In Heliopolis (the site of modern-day Cairo), people did not attribute creation to the god Ptah. They believed that Atum was the creator god who gave rise to the other gods. About 150 miles farther south in Hermopolis the creation gods consisted of a group of eight called the Ogdoad (think of the word "octet" meaning eight). These eight gods gave rise to Atum, who, in turn, created people and animals.

Finally, the people in Thebes (location of the capital during New Kingdom Egypt) focused on one god of the eight gods, Amun. Long associated with the sun, Amun became known as the first creator god or "the First One who gave birth to the first ones."

From all of these different belief systems, the basic beliefs might be summarized by the following ideas.

- In the beginning was Chaos. From Chaos came nothingness called Nu. Somehow Amun came out of Nu. This is not really explained, but only referred to as a "mystery."

- Amun rose in the sky and became associated with the sun; he is also known as Ra. Actually the sun god may be referred to by some or all of these names—Amun, Ra, or Amun-Ra.

- From Amun-Ra came Air and Rain (Shu, Neftut), and Sky (Nut) and Earth (Geb).

- From Sky and Earth come four other gods—Osiris, Isis, Seth, and Nephthys.

- Osiris is the most important god and is considered good. The story of his creation, destruction, death, and rebirth is an important creation story. It is included in many collections of Egyptian mythology.

- Osiris is destroyed by his brother Seth but is helped and brought back to life, at least in an eternal way, by Isis. Isis is both wife and sister to Osiris. Their son, Horus, actually avenges the evil that Seth has done. Because these gods are not human in any form, we cannot really think of them as sisters and brothers in a human way. This may be difficult for children to ponder, but the educator can refer to the story as a "mystery."

- In addition to the birth-death-rebirth story of Osiris, other stories tell about Amun-Ra choosing gods to perform tasks for him. The god of Destiny is said to create humans on a divine potter's wheel.

- Egyptian gods, unlike Greek and Roman gods, do not stay in one place or always look like the same animal. The goddess Hathor, for example, is sometimes associated with the cow and other times with a lioness. It some accounts, Sekhmet, the Lioness Goddess, is later transformed into a cow and given the name "Hathor."

- Universal patterns in Egyptian mythology include these themes: life and death, mother as comforter, sun as life force, and water as renewal and destruction.

Bibliography

Angeletti, Roberta. *Nefertari, Princess of Egypt.* Oxford University Press, 1998.

This picture book fantasy tells the story of a girl named Anna who visits tombs in the Valley of the Queens. While in one of the tombs, Anna meets Nefertari, who has come alive to inform the girl about life in ancient Egypt. Some references to various gods makes this book suitable to include in this bibliography, and it is a delightful story to read aloud to students.

Cole, Joanna. *Ms. Frizzle's Adventures, Ancient Egypt.* Illustrated by Bruce Degen. Scholastic, 2001.

Most of this book concerns the popular teacher, Ms. Frizzle, and her students who take an airplane flight to Egypt and return to ancient times. Basic information is given about Egyptian life and burial practices, but brief references to various gods appear in sidebars. This appealing story, like the other School Bus books, will entertain children and can be shared as a read-aloud book, too.

Forty, Jo. *Ancient Egyptian Mythology.* Chartwell Books, 1996.

The first chapters give a history of Egypt and discuss religion, mummification, and burial practices. The majority of the book describes Egyptian gods and goddesses in detail, and the information is presented in alphabetical arrangement. Numerous photographs of archeological remains and a chronology of the dynasties appear at the end of the book.

Harris, Geraldine. *Gods and Pharaohs from Egyptian Mythology.* Illustrated by David O'Connor. Peter Bedrick Books, 1981.

This weighty volume begins with a history of Egypt and the importance of religion. Many legends of the gods are retold in detail, and the symbolism of the gods is explained. Older elementary students as well as high school students interested in the topic will find this source invaluable. Line drawings and full-color paintings add to the spirited text.

Hart, George. *Ancient Egypt.* Knopf, 1990.

One of the Eyewitness Books, this volume covers in brief more than twenty-five topics; one topic is devoted to Egyptian gods. Although the information in the text is limited, the many photographs add to children's understanding of this topic.

Keenan, Shelia. *Gods, Goddesses, and Monsters: A Book of World Myth*ology. Scholastic, 2000.
  This book is divided into countries and areas of the world, with ancient Egypt as one of fifteen short sections. Information on the gods is provided in an alphabetical arrangement.

Morley, Jacqueline. *Egyptian Myths*. Illustrated by Giovanni Caselli. Peter Bedrick Books, 1999.
  The author's modern, long retelling of eleven myths can be retold or read aloud to older elementary-age students. Beautifully painted illustrations and attractive formatting add to the elegance of the stories and understanding of the Egyptian civilization.

Murray, M. A. *Legends of Ancient Egypt*. Dover, 2000.
  The legends in this book are told in a straightforward fashion and were used in recounting the specific stories for this chapter. This book is less complicated than the one by Geraldine Harris.

Nardo, Don. *Egyptian Mythology*. Enslow, 2001.
  Detailed, informative text explains basic beliefs of the ancient Egyptian civilization with eight myths and notes. A useful question-and-answer format and expert commentary follows each section.

Perl, Lila. *Mummies, Tombs, and Treasure: Secrets of Ancient Egypt*. Clarion, 1987.
  This popular book gives a wealth of information about ancient Egypt and belongs in any library. It has numerous references to the different Egyptian gods.

Tiano, Oliver. *Ramses II and Egypt*. Holt, 1996.
  In addition to information about Pharaoh Ramses II, useful information about ancient Egypt and the universe of Egyptian gods is provided.

Egypt in the Very Beginning: A Program for Schools

This school program involves student research, writing, and storytelling of basic Egyptian myths. In addition, students can use the script "Great Sun, Great River" in a reader's theatre production. Turn this production into a full-fledged production with large stick puppets (see designs in this chapter) carried in a reenactment of a funeral procession. Art and music students can make these props and find musical tapes to add to the mood of the story.

Although we have no written music (or recordings!) of how the ancient music sounded, some music samples that try to give a flavor of it are available. Web sites such as this one can guide teachers: www.aldokan.com/mp3/mp3.htm. Another possibility is to have students shake rattles and create sound effects to accompany the chants in the script provided.

Materials Needed

1. Five white poster boards

2. Five paint sticks or five two-foot dowels

3. Loose-leaf notebook

4. Tan watercolor paper

5. Artificial palm fronds or ornamental grass

Procedure

1. Using the brief summaries of sample myths, instruct students to retell the stories. They may choose to write out stories in straight narrative form, or they may wish to make a script in the manner of "Great Sun, Great River." If the script method is used, designate narrators to describe the setting and "set the scene." The majority of the story is then told through dialogue.

2. Before students begin their script writing and retelling, you will want them to know something about the ancient Egyptian civilization. Those library media specialists and teachers who include a unit on ancient Egypt will already have established a format for providing this background. In other cases, the teacher/librarian may consult the bibliography in this chapter for basic source materials about Egypt.

3. Make a display of the Egyptian books and story collections in your library to whet students' appetites for this project. Include objects such as media kits and realia available in bookstores and educational materials stores. If your community does not have these resources, search the Internet for materials. Two Web sites are listed in this chapter's introduction.

4. Compile a notebook or scrapbook of the myths your students write. Student artists can provide paintings on papyrus purchased in an art store or on tan watercolor paper. The paintings can show typical tomb paintings of Egyptian gods or scenes from the myths as students visualize the stories.

5. Stage a production of student scripts or the story "Great Sun, Great River." Use the suggestions preceding the script for readers and movement to turn this script into a pageant in the manner of a funeral procession. The story itself calls for some readers to speak the dialogue and other students to carry the large stick puppets of the gods Osiris, Isis, Seth, Horus, and Anubis. You can easily include other students or an entire class by assembling a "chorus" to chant the chorus lines. Another way to include more children is to designate some students to carry palm fronds, sheaves of wheat, or ornamental grass and wave as the procession moves into the classroom or around the library.

Sample Myth Summaries

Ra, the All Seeing Eye, and Hathor, the Goddess of Love

In the beginning there was Nu, the vast ocean. From this vast ocean, a voice came forth to say, "I am Ra, the All Seeing One." Ra had many names and was worshipped by the other gods and the people upon the earth.

One day, Ra looked upon his land and saw that there were people who were leading shameful lives. They were not speaking his name with respect. Ra asked the God Nu to advise him what should happen to the people on earth.

Nu spoke that people should always respect Ra. If he allowed this behavior to continue, Ra's power would be lessened. Nu told Ra to send out his powerful eye upon the land to seek out the disobedient. The disobedient should then be destroyed.

Ra did this. He found the disobedient people, but he himself did not wish to destroy any creature on the earth. Instead, Ra sent out the Lion Goddess Sekhmet to devour those people. Sekhmet began to destroy and devour people. Before long, she developed a taste for blood and the destruction grew and grew.

Ra feared for all people upon the earth as blood poured across the land. Once again Ra consulted Nu who put the idea in Ra's head to trick Sekhmet.

As in a dream, Ra awoke with the plan to send forth messengers to find large supplies of barley grain to make beer. Then Ra sent forth another messenger to bring back red clay soil from the land to dye the beer red. Finally, royal beer makers took their brew to the Goddess Sekhmet and told her this was a new kind of blood to satisfy her thirst.

When Sekhmet drank the new beer, she found it so delicious that she drank and drank until she fell into a deep stupor. When she awoke, she no longer remembered why she had destroyed people, and she was no longer thirsty for blood.

Then, in the peaceful days that stretched ahead, Ra called Sekhmet to his royal temple. He changed her from the Lioness into a more peaceful creature, a cow. He changed her name to Hathor, which means "Love." In this way, love reigned upon the earth, and people celebrated this transformation every year at the Festival of Hathor, Goddess of Love.

The Scorpions of Isis

Now after the evil Seth destroyed Osiris the first time, Isis the sister of Osiris and Seth was living in grief. The Ibis headed God of Wisdom, Thoth, came to comfort Isis. He warned her that she should flee lest Seth destroy her, too. He advised her to take along seven scorpions to protect her as she traveled.

Isis took the scorpions with her and instructed some of the scorpions to travel ahead and other scorpions to walk beside her. They walked and walked until one day they came to the house of a woman living in the marshes. The woman's house was grand and filled with gold and precious stones.

Isis wished to rest at this woman's house. But the woman was afraid of the scorpions, so she denied Isis's request. Isis was tired from her journey but traveled on until she came to the house of another woman living in the marshes. This woman was very poor, but she was brave and willing to let Isis rest in her house.

Isis rested. While she rested, the scorpions decided to teach the rich marsh woman a lesson. They gathered all of their venom together and gave it to Tefen, the largest scorpion. Tefen went to the first woman's house, crept under the doorway, and stung the woman's infant son.

The woman's cries and laments awakened Isis. The heavens of their own accord sent down fire and floods upon the woman's house. Isis went to the woman's house where she saw the lifeless infant at his mother's breast. Isis heard the woman's cries. She took pity on the woman. The fires and floods spread to the houses of other innocent people.

Isis told the rich woman to take some of her gold and precious stone to the house of the poor marsh woman and distribute these to others in the land. The rich woman did as she was asked. In this way, Isis persuaded the Heavens to stop the fires and floods. Isis used her magic spells to draw the scorpion's poison out of the infant son. In this way, the baby was saved.

The child recovered, and from then on, all people knew they would be comforted in their miseries by the good Goddess Isis.

Great Sun, Great River

Program Note

This script is intended to be read as the narrators and five gods with the "standard bearers" carrying the stick puppets walk or process into the room. Other children will dangle the smaller scorpion stick puppets from long thin dowels as they surround Isis at the appointed time in the story. The procession ends where the first asterisk appears in the script.

The readers then stand in front of the room as Osiris speaks his first line. Osiris steps forward to read his line, then Seth steps forward to read his line. When Seth invites Osiris to his house, the two characters move to one side of the room. When Narrator II tells the audience that Seth throws the trunk into the river, Osiris turns his back away from the audience to indicate that he has been destroyed.

Then Isis steps forward to address the audience. She moves to the place where Osiris is "hiding," and together they move to the center of the room. Seth moves to the center of the room when he vows to kill Osiris the second time. The readers pause when this happens in the story, after the line "Egypt was a land of woe" is given by the second narrator. Osiris then moves to the back of the room in silence.

When Isis asks, "Who can help me find my good brother?" she walks around the room to where Anubis is standing. Together Anubis and Isis move to Osiris. Then Anubis makes grand gestures around Osiris to suggest the power of embalming. Isis mimics the gestures of Anubis to suggest she is helping with the embalming.

After Narrator III's line "Mourners cried," all the characters move to the front of the room as the play is finished.

Add music and props as you like. Patterns for the large stick puppets of the gods are included in this chapter. Smaller scorpions can be made and attached to long dowels as they hover around Isis to protect her. The chorus of students reading the choral lines may wear ceremonial collars or armbands as described later. Other students may wave palm fronds or ornamental grass.

The Script: Great Sun, Great River

Narrator I: Long ago, very long ago in Egypt

Narrator II: In the land of great desert

Narrator I: A great river, the Nile River

Narrator II: Swept across the land.

Narrator I: And every year, once each year, the river flooded the land.

Narrator III: The land turned to mud, and the mud that was left behind was good

Narrator IV: For in that mud, farmers grew barley and wheat

Narrator III: Farmers grew beans and lentils, garlic and leeks.

Narrator IV: There were figs and dates and grapes.

Narrator III: Antelope and lions ran wild.

Narrator IV: People hunted and fished, built homes, and had families

Narrator I: Beside the river, the great river

Narrator II: That swept across the land

Narrator I: And flooded the land each year.

Narrator III: And in Egypt there was sun, desert sun

Narrator IV: A great sun, a hot sun.

Narrator III: Sun caused wheat to wither and die

Narrator IV: Sun could bring life, sun could bring death

Narrator III: River could bring life, river could bring death.

Chorus: Great Sun, Great River. * [Movement of the procession ends as everyone then stands in the front of the room to continue the play reading.]

Narrator I: In this land of Egypt, there was once a king, a pharaoh, a god on earth—

Osiris: I am Osiris, a king, a god, ruler of this land. My people are a great people. For me they have built temples and grow vineyards. For me they raise cattle and prepare feasts. For me they bring gold and treasures. My land is a wealthy land. My people are content.

Chorus: O great land! O great Osiris! O great and good god of this land!

Narrator I: But all was not well in the land of Egypt for Osiris had a brother

Narrator II: A jealous brother, an evil brother.

Chorus: (*warning*) A jealous brother is an evil brother. O beware, Osiris.

Seth: I am Seth, handsome as Osiris, strong as Osiris, great as Osiris. If only I had the power of Osiris. This land could be my land. Then people would build temples for Seth. Gold temples for Seth.

Narrator I:	One day Seth invited Osiris to a feast in his home.
Seth:	Come, Osiris. Come, brother of mine. Come to a banquet in your honor. I shall have wine and cakes, plucked geese, the head of a calf, and the heart of the finest ox in the land.
Osiris:	You do me honor, indeed, brother. I shall come.
Chorus:	O, Osiris, beware! Seth is jealous. He means great harm!
Narrator I:	But Osiris was a trusting god. He went to the banquet. He feasted on wine and cakes
Narrator II:	He feasted on goose and calf.
Narrator III:	While he was feasting, Seth dazzled him with splendid jewels
Narrator IV:	Seth put magic spells on the wine and gave the enchanted drink to his brother, Osiris.
Narrator I:	And when Osiris fell into a deep sleep, Seth put him in a trunk and threw the trunk into the river
Narrator II:	The great river, the Nile River.
Chorus:	O woe! River of Life has become the River of Death. Osiris, good Osiris Dead. Dead in the Nile River. Woe. Egypt is a land of woe.
Seth:	I shall rule the land of Egypt. People of Egypt, bow before the all-powerful Seth!
Chorus:	O, Egypt Land of Woe. Shall no one comfort the land of Egypt?
Isis:	I am Isis, sister of Osiris. My brother is good. I shall find Osiris in the river. I will bring him back. Seth will not triumph as long as I can find my brother.
Chorus:	Look in the river In the dark places of the Nile River Use your magic eye, Isis, Use your eye to find the trunk Where Seth has hidden Your good brother, Osiris.
Narrator I:	Isis looked far and deep into the Nile River.
Narrator II:	And so she found the trunk.
Narrator III:	In the trunk she found Osiris.
Narrator IV:	She brought back her brother from death to life.
Narrator I:	Just as the Nile River floods the land each year

Narrator II:	Bringing the desert land back to life.
Narrator III:	Isis brought Osiris back to life.
Narrator IV:	Egypt was a land of plenty. The people rejoiced.
Chorus:	O great Land. O great Isis. Thanks to Isis for bringing back the good Osiris. O good Osiris of our good land!
Narrator I:	But Seth saw what Isis had done.
Narrator II:	Evil Seth
Seth:	I will not have my brother back. He was dead, and dead he will be.
Narrator III:	Evil Seth had a plan.
Narrator IV:	Seth came to Osiris when he was asleep.
Narrator III:	Seth dismembered him.
Narrator IV:	Seth cut the body of Osiris into pieces
Narrator I:	Fourteen pieces
Narrator II:	Seth took the fourteen pieces and scattered them far and wide throughout the land of Egypt.
Chorus:	O woe be Egypt. Land of death!
Isis:	Where is my brother? Where is Osiris? Who can help me find my good brother?
Chorus:	Who can help the brave Isis?
Narrator I:	Anubis, the god of the underworld came to Isis
Narrator II:	Anubis, protector of the dead, came
Anubis:	Dear Isis, I have come to help you find your brother. First you send out your eye upon the lands. I will bring scorpions to protect you. Look and when you have found the sacred parts of your brother, bring them to me.
Narrator III:	Isis did as she was told.
Narrator IV:	Scorpions came to watch over her
Narrator I:	Isis traveled to the north and south of the land.
Narrator II:	Isis found the sacred parts of her brother and took these back to Anubis. [Anubis and Isis move to Osiris.]
Isis:	Here is my brother. But what can I do with these sacred parts?
Anubis:	You are the maker of enchanted spells. Breath your magic upon the parts.
Isis:	Osiris, brother, god, good god become whole with my words become Osiris.
Anubis:	I shall now teach you the way of embalming. Wash his body in the Nile River.

Narrator III:	The washing was a sign of rebirth.
Anubis:	Put oil upon his body, wrap his limbs in cloth. Give him amulets. Open his mouth so that he may speak again.
Narrator IV:	Isis spent forty-five days performing these tasks so that her brother Osiris would live again in the next life.
Narrator I:	The people went with her.
Narrator II:	The people played music.
Narrator III:	Mourners cried.
Narrator IV:	The people carried the good Osiris to the land of the afterlife where he could live again.
Chorus:	O great Osiris. Come again year after year At the time of the flooding Come bring us life again.
Narrator I:	Then with the help of all the gods Isis gave birth to a son.
Narrator II:	The son Horus.
Narrator III:	Horus grew strong.
Narrator IV:	Horus became a man, and one day he vowed to avenge Osiris.
Horus:	I am Horus. I am the mystical son of Osiris. With magic spells and the strength of all the gods I will kill Seth.
Narrator I:	The evil Seth had no protector, no help in the land of Egypt. But Horus was strong. Horus had the help of all the good gods.
Narrator II:	With the power of all the gods, Horus killed Seth.
Narrator III:	Once again, peace came to the land of Egypt.
Narrator IV:	Horus like the sun took his father's place.
Narrator I:	Plants grow.
Narrator II:	Plants die.
Narrator III:	The river comes.
Narrator IV:	Plants grow again.
Narrator I:	What happens to plants can happen to people.
Narrator II:	Life and death.
Narrator III:	Life after death.
Narrator IV:	The story of Osiris is the story of ancient Egypt, land of birth. and death and rebirth.
Chorus:	Great Sun, Great River.

Egypt—Door to the Ancient World:
A Program for Public Libraries

This program combines games involving Egyptian mythology with related craft projects to use in a public library setting. Some libraries may also wish to use the script "Great Sun, Great River" in their programs by assigning a teen drama group to reenact the play for younger children. Because most public libraries offer single-event programs, this simplified plan will answer that need. If the library plans an entire summer program around ancient Egypt, the story summaries for the school program could be used for other events. In addition, the chapter "Mummy" from my earlier book *Fanfares* (Libraries Unlimited, 1990) contains a variety of Egyptian activities from a tour through a library set up as if it were an ancient Egyptian burial chamber to creating wall murals and making paper mummy cases.

Materials Needed

1. Egyptian posters, if desired

2. Rubber stamps of Egyptian hieroglyphics, if desired

3. Egyptian stickers or chocolate coins wrapped in golden paper for prizes

4. Colored construction paper and photocopies of armbands

5. Heavy white paper and photocopies of ceremonial collars

Procedures

1. In preparation for this program, the librarian may want to display pictures of ancient Egyptian Gods. Many posters and prints can be purchased in book stores, but librarians can also print drawings from the Internet. These two sites are helpful:

    www.rom.on.ca/egypt/case/about/gods.html

    www.ancientegypt.co.uk/gods/home.html

    As children arrive at the program, give each one a nametag to wear. For added fun, provide rubber stamps of hieroglyphics or Egyptian designs for kids to decorate the tags. Children may want to draw a picture of one of the gods from the wall display on their tags and choose to be that god for the day instead of using their own name.

2. Divide the group into teams of two or three to answer one or two questions in the area of Egyptian mythology and lore. Sample questions are provided in this chapter. Make a display of library books about Egypt for kids to find the answers. Set a time limit of about fifteen minutes to complete this work. The leader then reads questions aloud with each team responding with the answers they have researched. All participants receive a small prize such as an Egyptian sticker or chocolate coins wrapped in golden paper.

3. Escort children to craft tables set up with art supplies listed in the materials list above. Children may make a ceremonial collar and an armband.

4. End program by telling an Egyptian folktale or reading a book such as *Nefertari, Princess of Egypt* by Roberta Angeletti.

Egyptian Smart: A Game to Test Kids' Knowledge about Ancient Egypt

1. Which Egyptian god is associated with the sun?

2. Name the two gods who produced Osiris and his sister Isis.

3. Why was the southern part of Egypt called Upper Egypt and northern Egypt called Lower Egypt?

4. What animal's head is associated with the god of the Underworld?

5. What creature supposedly shoved the sun across the sky in the morning?

6. Who put Osiris's body in a trunk and then threw it in the river?

7. What bird is associated with the Egyptian god of writing and wisdom?

8. Which goddess is associated with love?

9. What color was associated with death in ancient Egypt?

10. What was Horus's main accomplishment?

11. Why was mummification so important to the ancient Egyptians?

12. What is meant by "the red land"?

13. What is meant by "the black land'?

14. What is an ankh?

15. Which Egyptian god is associated with embalming?

16. Which animals were thought to be sun worshippers because they shouted at sunrise and sunset?

17. Why was papyrus important to the ancient Egyptians?

18. Name one musical instrument that was used by ancient Egyptians.

19. In what kind of vehicle was the body of the pharaoh transported to the next world?

20. Name one animal that was mummified by the ancient Egyptians.

Answers to "Egyptian Smart"

1. Ra or Aten or Amun

2. Earth or Geb and Sky or Nut

3. The Nile River flows from south (Upper Egypt) to north (Lower Egypt), thus the headwaters or beginning was considered "upper."

4. The jackal head of Anubis

5. The scarab beetle

6. Seth

7. The ibis or Thoth

8. Hathor

9. Green

10. He avenged Osiris's death by killing Seth

11. It preserved the body for the afterlife

12. The desert

13. The fertile land around the Nile River

14. The symbol of long life

15. Anubis

16. Baboons

17. They made paper from this plant

18. Lyres, sistrums, drums

19. A funerary boat

20. Cats, crocodiles, bulls

Art Projects for Egyptian Mythology

Egyptian God Stick Puppets

Enlarge the patterns of Osiris, Isis, Anubis, Seth, and Horus to about one-half poster size (about 16 x 20 inches). These puppets need to be mounted or drawn on heavy stock, at least as heavy as light-weight poster board so they will be rigid when mounted on sticks. Leave the figures plain black and white or color them if you wish. For authenticity, check color illustrations or photographs in the books on Egypt to use the traditional ancient color scheme. Cut out puppets, and tape a paint stick or flat piece of balsa wood to the back of each figure so they can be carried in the procession of "Great Sun, Great River."

Children may want to make smaller versions of these Egyptian gods during the school or public library programs described in this chapter.

Figure 4.1. Osiris

Figure 4.2. Isis

Figure 4.3. Anubis

Figure 4.4. Seth

Figure 4.5. Horus

Egyptian Armbands and Ceremonial Collars

For armbands, cut strips of construction paper about 3 x 12 inches. Photocopy the patterns found on this page, color if desired, and glue onto armband strips. Measure strip to child's upper arm and tape to size. The armband should fit comfortably enough to take on and off. Artistic children may prefer to draw their own Egyptian hieroglyphic symbols on the bands. These samples and examples of the Egyptian hieroglyphics found in books may be displayed.

For ceremonial collars, photocopy the pattern shown in Figure 4.7 and supply children with markers to decorate the collars as they wish. Enlarge collar pattern as desired.

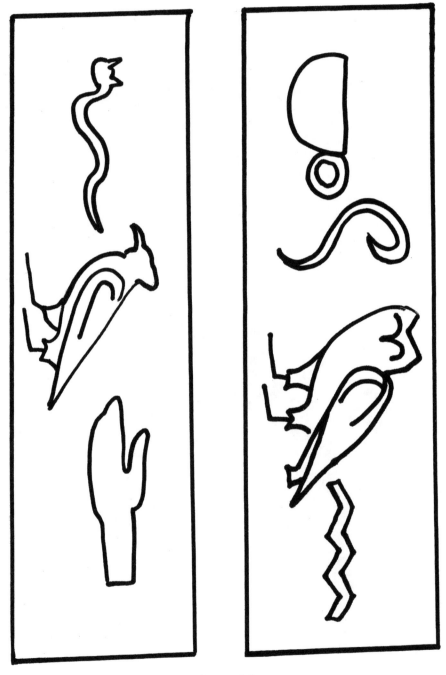

Figure 4.6

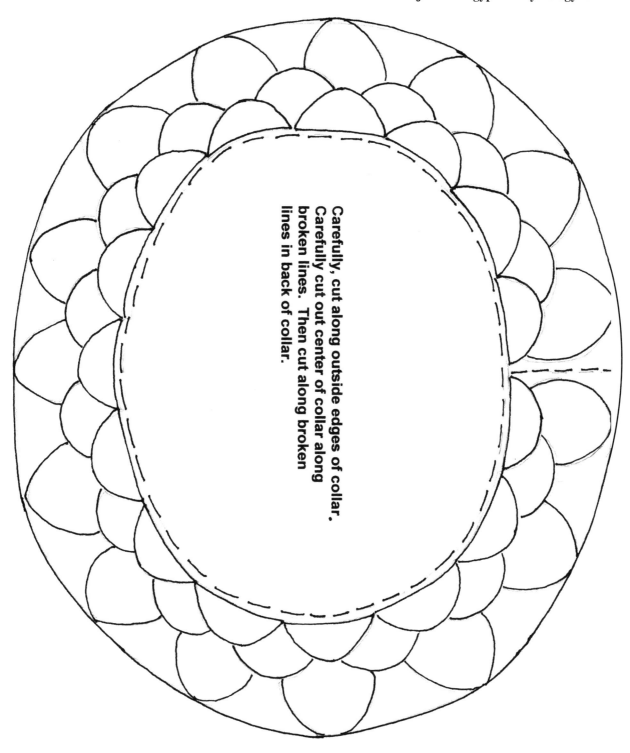

Carefully, cut along outside edges of collar. Carefully cut out center of collar along broken lines. Then cut along broken lines in back of collar.

Figure 4.7

Brains and Bravery in Folk Literature

Children growing up today are unaware of the big breakthrough twenty-five years ago in children's books. Those of us who experienced this turning point began to read books differently. Previously, library shelves were filled with a plethora of passive princesses–conquering hero storybooks. These shallow tales were further sanitized in books and animated films by the Disney studios. But in the 1970s, bibliographies noting strong female characters and folktale collections with active heroines opened our eyes to stories long forgotten or not previously explored. "Little Miss Muffet Strikes Back" was the model for feminist bibliographies and collections such as Rosemary Minard's *Womenfolk and Fairy Tales* guided us in building stronger library collections.

Since the 1970s, publishers have sought stories with strong girls and turned to a wider variety of folk tales not previously published. With the demand for multicultural stories, publishers added *Yeh-Shen* from China, *The Turkey Girl* from the Zuni people, and *The Rough-Face Girl* from Algonquin Indian folklore to the Cinderella stories collected by Perrault that had more or less been "the standard version" up until then. Times had changed. Well-educated children no longer thought of the girl with the glass slipper as the only princess in the realm.

But where did this leave the boys? What models for male heroes were brought to life? Unfortunately, there was not much of a breakthrough in book publishing and bibliographies for raising boys with a wide range of choices. Somehow publishers, parents, and too many educators saw little wrong with the physically strong, even macho man image for boys. Our culture still celebrates cowboys and tough men more than it appreciates quiet courage and steadfast behavior. Fortunately, the gifted writer Jane Yolen has compiled an outstanding collection of folktales for boys titled *Mightier than the Sword*. In her introduction, Yolen explains that a hero is a word for "winner, not whipper" and "picking up a sword" doesn't make a boy a hero, but "sticking to your word does." Further, she explains that she doesn't believe "one should never fight" but "true heroes are the ones who solve their problems—and the problems of the world—without ever having to resort to force. The tongue is mightier than the sword. As is the pen." Amen, Jane Yolen!

This chapter builds on Yolen's philosophy. "Brains and Bravery in Folktales" presents a bibliography of stories and story collections in which main characters use their wits, their clever thinking, and their courage to succeed. This cannot be a comprehensive list, but it introduces a different kind of hero. Some of the tales include feats of physical strength, but most show women and men winning through problem solving without the use of brute force. This new model is especially appropriate in light of our growing concern about bullying behavior in schools. See the chapter "Mind Your Manners" with its subtheme of bullying as an extension of this definition of hero. If we are truly bothered by bullies on the playground and, later, in the workplace, we will read children folktales about strong boys and girls who refrain from aggression. We will help children find better models through role-playing and having thought-provoking discussions in classrooms. The activities in this chapter call on students to create stories and engage in creative dramatics exercises that are consistent with the books listed in the bibliography.

Some librarians and educators may doubt that boys (and even girls) will identify with this new definition of hero. They could become fearful that kids might think they are not "cool." Others may misunderstand the very nature of folktales as simplistic stories set in "once upon a time" always ending "happily ever after." Since media games, cartoons, and graphic novels show kids so much violence, what difference can we make? Is it more important to build library collections around these "popular" items, offensive as they may be, than to choose materials of better quality and wiser choices?

There are no definitive answers for all of these concerns, but I hope that readers of this chapter learn more about the nature of folk literature. Jane Yolen's classic collection of essays, *Touch Magic,* reminds all of us about the more complex and nuanced folktales we may not have thought about much. I admit that quality of library collections has always meant more to me than simply giving kids what they want in large gulps to quickly satisfy appetites demanding instant gratification of the mind. Youth librarians in public libraries walk hand in hand with teachers and school media specialists as we all bear responsibility in guiding kids to stories and ideas they may miss on their own.

We all know that children too easily step into "pretty princess" and "fierce warrior" roles, but there is a place for some traditional tales of this kind. There needs to be a balance between some popular media and the books that will last beyond this season's hot trend. Children's librarians are in the business of guiding rather than simply locating books as a salesperson in a bookstore would do. Make a practice of showing parents *Yeh-Shen* and *The Turkey Girl* along with a Disney Cinderella book they request so that they just might stretch their thinking. Continue to look for tales about brave girls who venture out to awaken sleeping princes, and stories when height alone does not make a hero.

Bibliography

Ai-Ling Louie. *Yeh-Shen: A Cinderella Story from China.* Illustrated by Ed Young. Philomel, 1982.
   In this Asian Cinderella tale, a girl beseeches bones of a magic fish to change her rags into beautiful clothing so that she may attend the king's ball. In leaving the ball, she loses one golden slipper, and her clothes turn back into rags. She is united with the king in the end.

Barchers, Suzanne, ed. *Wise Women: Folk and Fairy Tales from Around the World.* Libraries Unlimited, 1990.
   Clever, courageous, and resourceful women meet danger and adventure in nearly fifty folktales. Well-known stories such as the English "Molly Whuppie" appear as well as lesser known ones such as the Hawaiian "The Woman in the Moon."

Batt, Tanya Robyn, collector. *The Fabrics of Fairytale: Stories Spun from Far and Wide.* Illustrated by Rachel Griffin. Barefoot Books, 2000.
   Among the tales with strong heroes appears "The Silk Brocade" from China in which an old woman loses a prize brocade she has woven. The eldest sons do not succeed in recovering it, but the brave youngest son performs several courageous feats to accomplish the task and bring happiness in the end. The fabric illustrations will inspire student artists to develop art projects and folk motifs to accompany other folktales they will encounter.

Courlander, Harold. *The Tiger's Whisker and Other Tales from Asia and the Pacific.* Henry Holt, 1995.
   This reprint of the 1959 collection includes more than two dozen tales, many with strong protagonists who succeed through bravery and wit. The signature tale, "The Tiger's Whisker," involves

a brave woman who seeks the help of a wise elder to change her husband's unloving behavior after he has returned from war. Patiently and courageously she obtains a tiger's whisker and then learns a deeper truth in the end.

Lurie, Alison, ed. *Clever Gretchen and Other Forgotten Folktales.* Crowell, 1980.
  Among the tales retold is one of my favorites, "The Sleeping Prince," in which a plucky princess sets off to the far corners of the world as she wears out a pair of iron shoes and faces a fierce lions to find a sleeping prince whom she then rescues.

Martin, Rafe. *The Rough-Face Girl.* Illustrated by David Shannon. Putnam's, 1992.
  With courage and belief in herself, the rough-faced girl succeeds in marrying the Invisible Being when her beautiful but cruel sisters do not. She faces the strong sister of the Invisible Being by passing her test of answering three difficult questions to be acceptable enough to marry the Invisible Being.

Minard, Rosemary, ed. *Womenfolk and Fairy Tales.* Houghton Mifflin, 1974.
  These eighteen well-chosen tales have all been retold by various respected writers. Among these are "Clever Grethel" by Walter de la Mare, "Cap o' Rushes" by Joseph Jacobs, and "The Woman Who Flummoxed the Fairies" by Sorche Nic Leodhas.

Norfolk, Bobby, and Sherry Norfolk. *The Moral of the Story: Folktales for Character Development.* August House, 1999.
  These master storytellers include several tales to entertain and teach values to children. Their focus on oral retelling and use of source notes will help students and teachers.

Pollock, Penny. *The Turkey Girl.* Illustrated by Ed Young. Little, Brown, 1996.
  This Zuni Indian version of Cinderella ends quite differently from the European tales. The young woman loses the trust of the turkeys that have helped her and sadly is alienated from the creatures forever. Soft pastel pictures by the award-winning Ed Young add to the poignant tale.

Sierra, Judy. *Wiley and the Hairy Man.* Illustrated by Brian Pinkney. Dutton, 1996.
  Wiley and his mother outwit the Hairy Man three times, and so the "conjure man" does not bother them again. A popular African American folktale from Alabama with strong scratchboard illustrations by Pinkney inspires student skits and folktale writing.

Yolen, Jane, ed. *Mightier than the Sword: World Folktales for Strong Boys.* Silver Whistle/Harcourt, 2003.
  More than a dozen tales with courageous and clever heroes fill this outstanding collection that belongs in every library. The stories range from the Chinese "Magic Brocade" and the African American "Knee High Man" to the Abenaki "Thick Head."

Yolen, Jane, ed. *Not One Damsel in Distress: World Folktales for Strong Girls.* Silver Whistle/Harcourt, 2000.
  Over a dozen tales with brave and clever heroines range from the Greek story of Atalanta and the Pirate Princess from Poland to the ever-popular English tale "Molly Whuppie."

Zelinsky, Paul O., ed. and illustrator. *Rumplestiltskin.* Dutton, 1986.
  The original story from the Brothers Grimm involves a Miller's daughter who cannot spin straw into gold without the help of a strange little man. To outwit him, the daughter sends her maid to discover the man's name. I used this version to retell the Rumplestiltskin story found in this chapter but changed the daughter into a more active protagonist.

Winning Ways in Folktale Days: A Program for Schools

This program may be used in classrooms or school libraries to teach folktales as a model for student writing. The teacher or librarian first reads at least three folktales from the selected bibliography in this chapter, then gives students one of the Folktale Starters. Students may complete their tales at home or during subsequent class sessions. At the end of this brief unit, students or the teacher reads the tales aloud for a Folktale Fest. The Fest may be a single class celebration or a schoolwide event for many classes.

Materials Needed

1. Food for the Fest (apple cider, bread, cheese, apples, oatmeal cookies)

2. Skit Kit materials, if desired (see public library program list)

3. Rolls of art paper or brown paper and markers for folk hero alternative art project

Procedure

1. The teacher/librarian reads a folktale from the bibliography. She or he leads a student discussion in which elements of characters and character types, plot action (main problem to be solved), other tasks to be accomplished, and the resolution are identified.

2. The teacher/librarian reads another folktale then leads another discussion as in Step 1.

3. Repeat Step 2 with a third folktale or folktales.

4. Teacher distributes the "Folktale Writing Model" sheet and discusses each step with students based on the three tales that have been read.

5. Students choose a folktale starter from the list provided here for their writing projects.

6. Students read their tales in class or the teacher/librarian selects several tales to read anonymously to the class.

7. As an alternative to Step 6, a group of teachers or older students serve as a "reading panel" to select the stories read aloud.

8. If the teacher/librarian desires, the school librarian plans a Folktale Fest. Displays of folktale collections are set up for students to check out of the library, photocopies of student tales are published for several classes to read the tales, and reenactments of one or more tales are performed. Some of the stories provided in the Skit Kits of this chapter could be used.

9. Select folk ballads and instrumentals of folk music to begin and end the fest.

10. Serve cider and "peasant" snacks such as homemade-style peasant bread purchased from a bakery, cheese, apples, and oatmeal raisin cookies.

Folktale Starters

1. In the old days when younger sons were forgotten there lived a widowed woman who sent her three sons out to slay a dragon. The two older sons got lost before the year was past. The dragon still terrified the king. Reluctantly, she sent out her youngest. He had no weapons, but he did have many clever thoughts in his head.

2. Once upon a time, an evil toad put a curse on the king's son. When the prince turned sixteen years old, he fell into a deep sleep at the stroke of midnight, and everyone else in the kingdom fell asleep as well. They might have remained in this state had not a strong, young princess from outside their kingdom heard the story. She set out to find this prince and awaken the kingdom.

3. In days gone by, a woman who had three sons set out to weave a tapestry of the best dream she had ever had. The weaver worked for a full year, then, just as she finished the tapestry, a strong wind blew through her window and carried it out the window and far away. The woman was overcome with grief. The two older sons tried to recover the tapestry, but they soon lost interest. Finally, the younger son set out.

4. Once upon a time, a dragon burned down the palace of the princess who lived inside. She was furious. She told the prince of a nearby kingdom what had happened, but he was not at all sympathetic. So the princess decided to go out to meet the dragon.

5. Long ago when wishes were magic there lived a girl who made a wish upon the first star in the sky on midsummer's eve. She wished that the morning glory vine growing on her little house would grow fast and huge until it reached a castle in the sky. She wished that she could climb that vine and find her fortune. Well, the vine grew, but when she climbed to the top, she met with a big surprise.

6. In a day gone by there lived a terrible giant who stole food and whatever else he wanted from everyone in the nearby village. Tall lads and braggarts said they would slay the giant, but no one could ever accomplish this task. One day, a very small boy heard his brothers tell about the giant. This small boy promised himself that on his next birthday, he would quietly leave the village to find the giant.

Folktale Writing Model

Note: Use this worksheet to plan your own hero folktale. Remember that most folktales are about everyday people. The hero or heroine tale has a main character who has a problem or situation to solve. Several tasks may need to be accomplished before the problem is solved. Move the action along quickly, build to a high point, then resolve the problem for a satisfactory ending.

Beginning of Tale

1. Main character (introduce the character in simple terms and focus on a single trait or two traits to define the character):

2. Describe the setting (use little description; think of typical places such as forests, villages, outside a castle wall, caves, oceans, or a kingdom):

3.   Introduce the main problem or situation (examples might include slaying a dragon, finding the treasure guarded by a giant, escaping from a monster in a cave, bringing home enough money to support a mother or father, facing a great fear):

Middle of Tale

4.   Outline the steps the main character must take to solve the problem (accomplishing three tasks or going to a series of places to seek help are two examples):

5.   Describe the main solution (or describe the climax/high point):

End of Tale

6.   Show how the hero solves the problem then end with a closing statement.

Storybook Heroes Like You and Me: A Public Library Program

Kids love hero stories but may not realize that most folktale heroes are everyday people who accomplish great things because of simple traits such as courage, perseverance, good thinking, and creative ideas. Wit is more important that force, and winners are not bullies in the kind of hero tales introduced in this program. The following procedure suggests several choices for your program.

Materials Needed

1.   Boxes for Skit Kits

2.   Skit Kit covers

3.   For "Knee High Man": twine and leaves, photocopies of masks

4.   Costumes for "Rumplestiltskin": knit stocking cap, two aprons, two paper crowns, three ribbon or scarf sashes, three headscarves or kerchiefs, a cloak or cape

5.   "Watch Your Time" (Cinderella story) costumes: ragged dress or T-shirt, jeans, holey socks, tinsel covered wire for halo headband, large package or roll of wide ribbon for sashes, two yards of fabric for capes, paint stick, Styrofoam ball, margarine tub, marker and ribbon for the silly watch.

6.   For "Molly Whuppie" costumes: one shawl, two headscarves or kerchiefs, large boots, four aprons, one paper crown, two ribbon sashes, ball of twine for three string necklaces, package of gold twine for necklaces, old purse, shower curtain ring (or a bubble gum machine kind of silly ring), one yard of fat yarn.

Procedure

1.   Prepare several Skit Kits based on the ideas provided below. You may develop some of the skits into a more complete script such as the "Knee High Man."

2. Ask volunteers and staff to help you work with children in small groups. Decide how many groups (and volunteers) you will need based on the number of characters given in directions and on your best guess of the number of children who will attend the program.

3. Plan additional Skit Kits as needed or simply read other folktales listed in this chapter's bibliography to additional groups of children. Guide the children to mime the story after you have read it a second time.

4. Plan time for skit practice (perhaps twenty to thirty minutes) and additional time for the groups to perform.

5. If you decide to simply have children do the skits in small groups, select a folktale to read or tell at the beginning and end of the program.

6. Serve snacks such as cider and peasant bread with cheese or cookies and punch.

Skit Kits

Provide children with Skit Kits to create their own folktale skits. Divide the group into smaller groups based on the number of characters designated on the Skit Cards. Assign a high school drama student or an adult to each skit group to guide children in creating skits. Consult the chapter on Creative Dramatics if you think a teacher/leader-style story theatre would be more successful than expecting children to make up their own production with improvised dialogue. I have included a fully developed story theatre script for "The Knee High Man." The other Skit Kits simply describe the story action but call for children to create their own dialogue and action.

Reproduce the following Skit Cards for each kit. Photocopy the Skit Kit cover sheet (Figure 5.1) to make an attractive cover for each script. In addition to the Skit Cards, assemble props and costumes suggested on the card, and package kits in large plastic bags with sealed closures or clear plastic totes or boxes.

Figure 5.1

Skit Kit I: Knee High Man

Characters: Knee High Man, Horse, Bull, Owl, Narrator

Narrator (N): In a swamp in the southern part of the United States some years ago lived a knee-high man. He was smaller than many animals. Knee high to a horse. Knee high to a bull. He was even knee high to a large dog. He was teensy, but he wanted to be big. One day he went to call on the big animals in the region. He walked and he walked until he saw Mr. Horse.

KH Man: Hey up there! Mr. Horse, I'm down here. I'm the Knee High Man. Can you see me? Down here by your knee!

Horse: Speak up, Man. You also have a knee-high voice.

KH Man: Put your head down, Horse. I'll try to talk as big as I can.

Horse: Well, alright. Oh, there you are! What do you want with me?

KH Man: I want to be as big as you are. How can I do that?

Horse: Hmm. I suppose you could eat a whole mess of corn. Maybe an apple and some hay. Just eat like I do. You know what they say? Hungry as a horse. Eat, Man!

KH Man: Thanks a lot!

N: So Knee High Man ate and he ate. He ate one dozen ears of corn, six apples, and a wheelbarrow full of hay.

KH Man: Oooooo! My belly aches. But I am not any taller. Maybe Bull can help me. I shall visit him.

N: So he walked and he walked and he walked until he saw Mr. Bull.

KH Man: Mr. Bull! Hey there, Mr. Bull. I'm down here. Can you see me?

Bull: I don't see you. Are you playin' a game with me?

KH Man: Mr. Bull, I'm Knee High Man! Just look down to your knees.

Bull: Man, you are knee high to a grasshopper, aren't ya?

KH Man: Yes, I am sorry to say I am.

Bull: Well, what do you want from me?

KH Man: Tell me how I can be big like you.

Bull: Big like me? That's not easy to do. Are you sure?

KH Man: Oh yes. I'll do anything!

Bull: Eat grass. Lots and lots of grass.

N: So Knee High Man went off to the pastureland. He ate and he ate And he ate. Three barrows full of grass.

KH Man: Ooooo! My belly aches. If I eat one more bite, I'll pop. And look at me! I haven't grown one inch. What shall I do? I know! If anyone can help me, it's Owl. Owl is wise. I shall visit Owl.

N: So Knee High Man walked and he walked until he came to an old oak tree where Owl lived.

KH Man: Hellooooo Mr. Owl. Helloooo up there!

Owl: Whoooooo are you?

KH Man: I am Knee High Man. I am knee high to a grasshopper. I'm way down here at the root of your tree.

Owl: What do you want from me?

KH Man: I am tired of being small. Please tell me how I can be big.

Owl: How big?

KH Man: Just big. Big like Bull or Horse.

Owl: Are the animals horsing around with you? Are they bullying you?

KH Man: No.

Owl: Do you want to pick up big things?

KH Man: Not really.

Owl: Then you don't need to be any bigger. Size doesn't mean a thing. Unless you want to have a bigger brain. You seem plenty smart enough to me. You seem brave enough to ask me for advice. My advice is to think about it. You are fine the way you are. Good-bye!

N: So Owl flew off. Knee High Man thought.

KH Man: I am smart and brave and small. Maybe Owl has a point. Why do I need to be any bigger? Yes, I am fine the way I am.

N: So Knee High Man went back to the swamp and spent the rest of his days being happy just the way he was.

Notes on Staging: If you wish a backdrop for the swamp, stretch an eight- to ten-foot length of green or brown twine across a wall horizontally. Next tie five or six 6-foot lengths of green twine "vines" vertically from the first length. Make periodic knots in the twine and staple large green leaves to the vines if desired (see Figure 5.2).

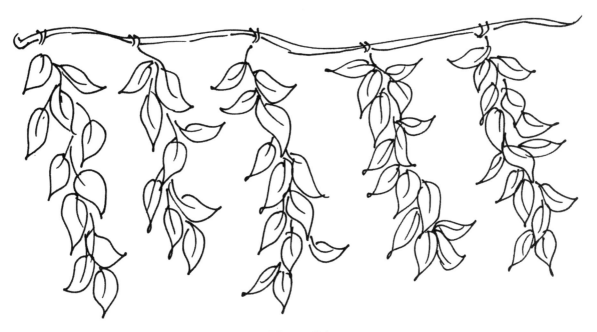

Figure 5.2

Use simple "costumes" to distinguish characters. The Knee High Man wears an oversized T-shirt. Reproduce the horse, bull, and owl masks illustrated in Figures 5.3–5.5 on card stock if desired, and attach to children's faces with thin elastic cording.

Figure 5.3. Horse

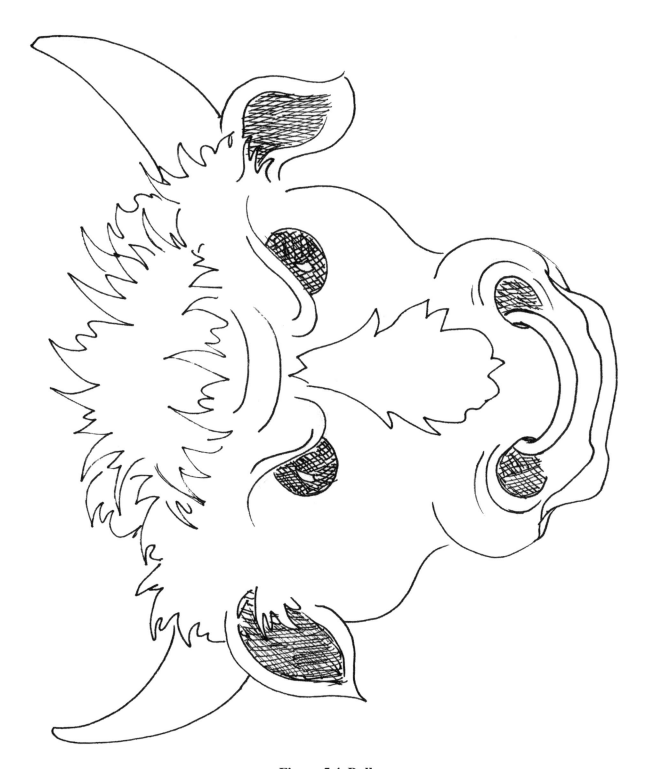

Figure 5.4. Bull

Figure 5.5. Owl

Skit Kit II: Rumplestiltskin Retold

(This version makes the miller's daughter an active heroine.)

Characters: The miller, mistress miller, the king, the king's herald, two servants of the king, Rumplestiltskin, maidservant to the princess, the baby (a doll wrapped in a blanket), three townswomen, the village storyteller

Plot: The king comes to town one day with his herald and servants. The town's miller vows to impress the king by telling him that his daughter can spin straw into gold. The king orders the daughter to come to court the next day.

At the palace, the king tells the girl she must spin a basket full of straw into gold by the next morning or die. After the king leaves, Mistress Miller cries. A bell rings, and a strange little man, Rumplestiltskin, appears. He agrees to spin the straw into gold for something in return. The little man works all night, and by morning has spun the straw into gold in return for Mistress Miller's necklace. The king wants more gold. He orders the girl to spin a huge bag full of straw into gold. The little man agrees to help, but asks for her whole jewelry box filled with jewels as the reward. The king then tells the girl he will marry her if she meets his final challenge to turn a whole room full of straw into gold.

When Rumplestiltskin arrives to help, he first asks what he will receive for such a large task. She says she has nothing left to give. He says he will help her if she gives him her first child to be born after she marries. The little man works twice as fast and spins all the straw in the room into gold.

The happy king marries Mistress Miller on the spot. They live happily for one year. At the end of the year, a baby is born to the new queen. One month later, the little man comes to take her baby away. The queen asks for another chance. The little man says she must guess his name in three days.

She makes a long list of every name she can think of. The next day, she guesses three names from the list. They are all wrong. The following morning she reads off six names, all of which are wrong. With one day left, the queen leaves her baby with the maidservant and sets out on a dangerous journey around the kingdom. She asks three women she meets at the well about the man. Next she visits the village storyteller, who says she has heard of a magic man but can only tell her where he might live, not with any certainty. The queen goes to the forest, hides behind a tree, and watches the man sing and dance. Then she overhears him tell his name. She returns to the palace ready to meet the little man at dawn. This time she announces his name as "Rumplestiltskin" and he yells that she cheated. But she remains firm, repeating his name three times. The little man then stomps his foot in anger and disappears never to be heard from again. The queen then receives her baby from the maid servant and goes to the king to tell him, "We will now live in peace the rest of our days."

Notes on Staging: If the four settings are important to designate, hang signs "Palace," "Town," "Forest" in different corners of the room. Simple costumes could include a knit stocking hat for the miller, an apron for Mistress Miller, a paper crown for the king, sashes for the king's servants and herald, headscarves for the women, a cloak for the village storyteller, an apron for the maidservant, and a crown for Mistress Miller when she marries the king.

Skit Kit III: Watch Your Time: A Silly Cinderella Tale

Characters: Sydney (male or female), magic person (male or female), royal person, assorted animals, people at the ball. Sydney and the royal person should be of the opposite sex.

Note about the Story: This silly tale is not so much a story in which a hero or heroine acts bravely or cleverly. Magic intervention happens but it isn't very successful, thereby telling us that tales often end with unforeseen conclusions. The "oh well" or "that's the way the cookie crumbles" ending seems to poke fun at those "happily ever after" expectations and to accept life as it is. This skit was originally published in *Straw into Gold* by Robin Currie and myself. I have made a few additions to the original skit outline.

Plot: Sydney is left alone when everyone else goes to the ball. A magic person appears and promises to help, but the magic is a little off base. Instead of changing mice to horses, they turn into camels. Various other problems with the magic occur (students can create the specifics). Through it all, Sydney is a good sport, either laughing or exclaiming, "Well, that's the way the cookie crumbles" as each mishap occurs.

Finally, Sidney, still dressed in rags but with a glittery cape, sets off for the ball. At the party, Sidney meets the royal person (prince or princess), forms a bunny-hop line and everyone has fun (dancing line dances, singing, and doing the actions to "YMCA" or whatever silly dances students can think of). Sydney suddenly looks at her wristwatch only to discover it's time to go. Her glittery cape disappears (students can brainstorm how this happens) at the ball.

The magic person runs into the ballroom and recites every magic spell she can think of. She waves her wand. She tells Sydney to turn around three times and click her heels. Nothing works. All guests at the ball try to think of ways for Sydney to improve her appearance without the cape. The hilarious suggestions (such as giving Sydney glittery tennis shoes, and sprinkling confetti in her hair) just make the royal person laugh harder. Finally, he asks Sydney to marry him so they will enjoy a fun life together. A quick wedding is performed, with the guests parading around with balloons and making noise with party horns.

Notes on Staging: Costumes include the following: a ragged dress or ragged T-shirt, jeans, and holey socks for Sydney; a glittery circle of stars or wire reinforced tinsel for the magic person; a robe for the royal person; a cape for Sydney; stuffed animals or puppets for the animals in story, wide ribbon to tie crossways from one shoulder to the waist for people at the ball. Make capes by taking a piece of fabric about sixteen to eighteen inches wide and thirty-six inches long (Figure 5.6). Fold over a heading of about one inch and stitch, staple, or tape this down to form a channel. Through this channel, run one yard of inexpensive ribbon or yarn to tie the cape around the neck of the royal person and Sydney at the ball. The glittery star or tinsel for the magic person can be purchased at discount or craft stores. Make a silly wand for the royal person from a yardstick or paint stick with a Styrofoam ball attached to one end. Make Sydney's watch face from the top of a plastic butter container. Write numbers on the blank side of the top with permanent magic markers. Attach clock hands with a brad fastener. Punch a hole in the watch face and tie it to the wrist with ribbon. Think of silly exaggeration for these and other props you may want to add.

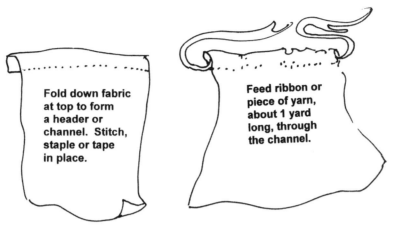

Fold down fabric at top to form a header or channel. Stitch, staple or tape in place.

Feed ribbon or piece of yarn, about 1 yard long, through the channel.

Figure 5.6

Skit Kit IV: Molly Whuppie

Characters: Molly Whuppie, Molly's sisters—older, and younger, a giant, the giant's wife, three daughters of the giant, the king, oldest son of king, second son of king, youngest son of king

Plot: Molly Whuppie and her two younger sisters are left in a dark wood because their parents cannot feed them any longer. Molly, a brave lassie, knocks at door of the giant's house and begs the giant's wife to take them in. The wife is reluctant but takes them in, when her giant husband stomps home. Molly and her sisters sleep in the loft along with the giant's daughters, but in the night the giant ties gold chains around his daughters' necks and straw around Molly's and her sisters' necks. Molly, only pretending sleep, exchanges the straw for the chains. Later the giant mistakenly batters his own daughters, goes to sleep, and Molly wakes her sisters so they can escape.

Molly tells the king what happened, and he beckons her to steal the giant's sword. If she is successful, her older sister can marry the king's eldest son. Molly steals the sword but awakens the giant, who chases her. She gets away because she lightly runs across a bridge made with one hair. The giant would never try that! Molly gives the sword to the king, who agrees to the promised marriage.

The king then beckons Molly to steal the giant's purse, and in return, he will marry his second son to Molly's younger sister. Molly returns to the giant's home, steals the purse, then runs back across the bridge. The king finally challenges Molly to steal the giant's ring, and, in return, he will give his youngest son to Molly in marriage.

As Molly is slipping off the giant's ring, he grabs her. Molly tricks him by telling him to put her in a bag with a dog, cat, needle, thread, and scissors. After the giant does this, Molly tricks the giant's wife to come inside the bag by cutting a hole then climbing out herself and sewing up the bag. The giant returns and beats the bag until his wife begs him to stop. Molly runs back across the bridge, presents the ring to the king, and marries his youngest son. They live happily ever after.

Note on Staging: Simple costumes consist of a shawl for Molly, kerchiefs for her two sisters, big boots for the giant, aprons for the giant's wife and three daughters, a crown for the king, and ribbon sashes for the king's sons.

Basic props include three string necklaces, three gold cord necklaces (using gift cording for presents), a toy sword or one made from cardboard, an old purse for giant's purse, and a big ring (the party-favor kind or a shower curtain ring for humorous effect), and a long piece of yarn for the bridge of one hair.

6

Child's Play: Creative Dramatics and Story Theatre

Teachers today might be concerned that the idea of creative dramatics itself takes too much time away from teaching basic skills and subjects in an already crowded curriculum. State standards and defined tests seem to leave teachers little wiggle room to do their jobs, let alone engage in activities that suggest creativity and play. Actually, activities in this chapter are brief, easy to include within the school curriculum, and satisfy state standards for oral expression. They can be adapted under a language arts curriculum and used to teach a social studies lesson or introduce a science concept. Teachers and librarians who have never been in a play or felt comfortable exploring drama will find exercises they can use immediately.

Children need opportunities to practice their powers of creativity beyond the hours spent in electronic game playing, reading stories, and taking tests over computers for comprehension. If we as educators are truly concerned about developing social skills, building self-confidence, and teaching cooperation, taking time to use some creative dramatics in schools will be well worth the effort.

Creative dramatics is a natural activity of young children. Their world of make believe and let's pretend blends along with a growing understanding of the world around them. Maurice Sendak's *Where the Wild Things Are* tells the story of Max, a wild child sent to bed without dinner for his disobedience. When Max is transported into an imaginary world, he becomes "King of the Wild Things." Wild Max in the real world is no different from the Max in his dream, but the imaginary world allows the boy to play out his role in a place where he is exalted, not punished. In the end, Max returns home, just as other children need to stretch limits within the safety net of a secure home where dinner is still waiting for them. This capstone book perfectly defines the world of "child's play," the subject of this chapter.

What is the difference between play, creative dramatics, and children's theatre? The lines are not always clear-cut, but a few definitions can help us explore this fascinating topic. The word "play" in this context refers to the natural state of children engaged in their own spontaneous world of role-playing. Grace, the imaginative child in Mary Hoffman's *Amazing Grace,* not only acts out stories her grandmother reads to her, but she effortlessly steps into a world of make believe. "Play" overlaps with playing games, but this chapter will not include games with strict rules nor the broader world of children's games from tag to checkers. Instead, some role-playing and theatre games appear.

On a continuum of less to more structured, "creative dramatics" may be defined as a form of drama in which children focus on the process of playing roles and expressing themselves rather than on formally presenting a finished product to an audience. "Participatory drama" uses some of the elements of creative dramatics but can become more structured when a "leader" actually reads or tells a story then asks children to "act out" the story in silent mime. Finally, the term "theatre" or "theater" refers to a play in which characters memorize lines to perform a story to an audience. (Incidentally, I prefer the French spelling "theatre" in American settings because I dislike hearing people pronounce the word as "The-A-ter.") This chapter does not cover this final step on the continuum, although readers' theatre scripts do appear in other chapters.

In reality, the lines between creative dramatics, theatre games, and participatory drama become fuzzy. When children are asked to "melt like an ice cube" or participate in a group mime in which everyone becomes a part of an imaginary perpetual motion machine, are they doing creative dramatics or participatory drama? Is a theatre game such as the popular "Mirror" exercise when two students face one another with one child mimicking the actions of the other an example of creative drama or participatory drama or just a "warm-up" for theatre? These academic questions need not disturb the teacher. The definitions provided here are simply meant to show the scope and kinds of dramatic possibilities to share with young people.

Creative dramatics and participatory theatre or "story theatre" (I sometimes use these two terms interchangeably) are excellent activities for elementary school–age children. Preschool children may be involved in simple drama of this kind as well. Usually "theatre" or line memorization is best for older students, although children gifted with dramatic talents may benefit from all forms of drama. In my experience, concentrating on line memorization, formal theatre "blocking" (stage movement from point A to point B), and full costumes can restrict children's imaginations. Kids can become so nervous from all the fuss that they fall into that age-old state of "stage fright" before they have explored the fun and benefited from a good drama experience.

Here, I share another cautionary note. Well-meaning teachers and librarians sometimes think they should "put on" school plays or invite audiences to watch a creative drama production. We all have seen dreadful examples of school plays when scared kids forget lines only to wilt in the wings. I have observed public library drama productions that should have just been informal creative dramatics exercises without inviting an audience to witness amateur players who try to "perform." Try story theatre in which kids mime or speak simple lines as a leader reads a story as an alternative approach or involve kids in readers' theatre by reading lines expressively. These two kinds of drama take less time to prepare and still engage kids in a form of drama.

There are not many sources using the search term "creative dramatics" or the term "story theatre." Story or theatre games yielded more references, but not as many as anticipated. By broadening the term to include storytelling and drama, the bibliography became more complete. The notes in this chapter's bibliography will guide librarians and teachers to the most appropriate materials available. Titles of storybooks to use in storytelling in different curricular areas appear under the school program description of this chapter.

This chapter provides some theatre games and warm-ups for students as well as drama suggestions to use in elementary schools. The "Drama Pyramid" with exercises will serve as a model for teachers and school librarians who may create additional pyramids to fit specific content areas. The "Day to Act Out" program designed for public libraries provides more opportunities to engage children in a creative dramatics workshop. This program, based on several I have done with library staffs in Iowa and Kansas, may become so popular in your library that you'll decide to start a drama group.

Bibliography

Bany-Winters, Lisa. *Funny Bones: Comedy Games and Activities for Kids.* Chicago Review Press, 2002.

Numerous skits and games will engage children in the kind of dramatic play to prepare them for more elaborate story theatre and creative dramatics activities. This text is specially useful for public libraries doing a creative dramatics workshop.

Hamilton, Martha, and Mitch Weiss. *Children Tell Stories: A Teaching Guide.* Richard C. Owens, 1990.

This is an outstanding storytelling book that also guides novice and experienced drama coaches. The warm-up exercises and pantomimes are especially helpful for the topic of creative dramatics.

Kohl, Mary Ann. *Making Make-Believe.* Gryphon House, 1999.

Most of the book is devoted to crafts, making puppets, and creating props for young children, but the simple props, costumes, and settings for creative play will be inspiring for primary grade students. The text features good, easy-to-follow instructions.

Lipman, Doug. *Storytelling Games: Creative Activities for Language, Communication, and Composition across the Curriculum.* Oryx, 1995.

Outstanding story games appropriate to use with children from preschool through high school. Directions are clear and complete with detailed indexes indicating the type of game and skills taught.

MacDonald, Margaret Read. *The Skit Book.* Linnet Books, 1990.

Many of this prolific author's storytelling books are also useful for story theatre, but this valuable book on skits will guide children in creating more than a hundred stories using creative dramatics techniques.

Rooyackers, Paul. *101 More Drama Games for Children.* Hunter House, 2002.

Exciting games clearly described will be helpful to educators and librarians, in particular because the author suggests appropriate grades and ages for each activity given. Introductory chapters provide solid reasons for using the games in educational settings.

Rubright, Lynn. *Beyond the Beanstalk: Interdisciplinary Learning through Storytelling.* Heinemann, 1996.

Most of this excellent guide treats storytelling as creative dramatics in that it involves children in creating stories and retelling them through an exploration of the senses involving movement and dramatic play. See especially the sections titled "Movement and Creative Dramatic Extensions."

Spolin, Viola. *Theater Games for Rehearsal: A Director's Handbook.* Northwestern University Press, 1985.

Warm-ups, tune-ups, and numerous creative games with side notes will guide teachers and librarians as they prepare young actors or simply use creative dramatics in the school or library.

Tip Sheet for Teaching Creative Dramatics

1. Try to remain flexible but establish order as the leader/facilitator.

2. Use at least one kind of control device such as striking a music note, hitting a drum, or raising one arm with two fingers pointed upward as in "listening ears." Children will then know to listen, "freeze action," or be ready for the next set of instructions.

3. Prepare activities with clear expectations so that children can move from the known to the more exploratory stage of discovery.

4. Think of individual, duo, and small-group team exercises. There are times when each is appropriate.

5. Teach respect by listening to children and asking them to listen to one another.

6. Warm up and cool down just as you might do in an exercise session.

7. Use only positive, constructive criticism.

8. Instead of "telling" children precisely what to do, involve them in thinking of alternative ways to express themselves. Also, show rather than tell. For example, "Might an old woman move like this . . . or like this [demonstrating possibilities]?"

9. Side coach or provide little ideas along the way, especially if students seem stymied and unable to proceed on their own.

10. Be prepared to set limits so that everyone will have a positive experience. For example, no profanity, vulgarity, or ugly behavior can be tolerated. Creative dramatics is not creative if children try to be scene-stealers or egocentric drama kings and queens.

The Drama Pyramid: A School Program of Creative Dramatics

School libraries or classroom teachers can use the ideas in this model to introduce creative dramatics into the curriculum. This activity can be used throughout the year or as part of a larger content area. The warm-up games begin the day's events with one of the more complex story theatre or creative dramatics activities following.

Materials Needed

1. At least one large poster board to make the pyramid

2. One pack of card stock in miscellaneous colors to make game cards

3. Markers, pens, and pencils

4. Props as needed

5. Index cards or writing pads to write out the activities

Procedure

1. Prepare the drama pyramid as directed below.

2. Introduce the idea of creative drama by giving children one or two of the warm-up games.

3. Read or tell a story then invite the children to participate in a retelling of the story through story theatre. Refer to the "Tip Sheet for Beginning Drama Coaches" if this is a new experience for you. *The Great Kapok Tree* (see section on science books later in this chapter) is an excellent choice for beginners, and it has the advantage of working well with almost all age groups, from kindergarten through middle school.

4. Teachers and librarians may wish to use ideas in this chapter throughout the school year. The Drama Pyramid lists more than twenty stories and story collections in various disciplines that can be adapted to the story theatre or creative dramatics experience. Students will remember factual information better if they can actively participate in this way.

The Drama Pyramid

Using the diagram in this chapter (Figure 6.1), create your own Drama Pyramid. The pyramid may be drawn on a white board or poster board with symbols to suggest different kinds of dramatic play and story theatre activities. Prepare playing cards with symbols to match the symbols on the board. The symbols are written on one side of the card with the proposed activity on the other side of the card (Figure 6.2).

Begin by choosing a creative play activity card or a warm-up game card for students to get started. Depending on your time, you may choose several WUG (warm-up game) cards.

Proceed with the next level of the pyramid by choosing a TLST (Teacher-Led Story Theatre) card. The teacher/librarian will read or tell a story proposed on the card. Students are urged to listen carefully because they will be helping the leader retell the story after the initial reading. Depending on the leader's wishes, students then participate by making sounds, adding actions, or taking parts in the story to mime or add speaking lines (or both).

Complete the drama pyramid by choosing a CDST (Creative Drama/Story Theatre) card. Some of these activities only give a title or opening line. This challenges children to do improvisational theatre as they invent dialogue, a plot line, and action spontaneously. Other CDST cards give children a more fleshed-out plot that they can act out and use their own words to tell the story. The easiest CDST cards give kids the title of a book that they can read and adapt to perform in their own way.

The Drama Pyramid

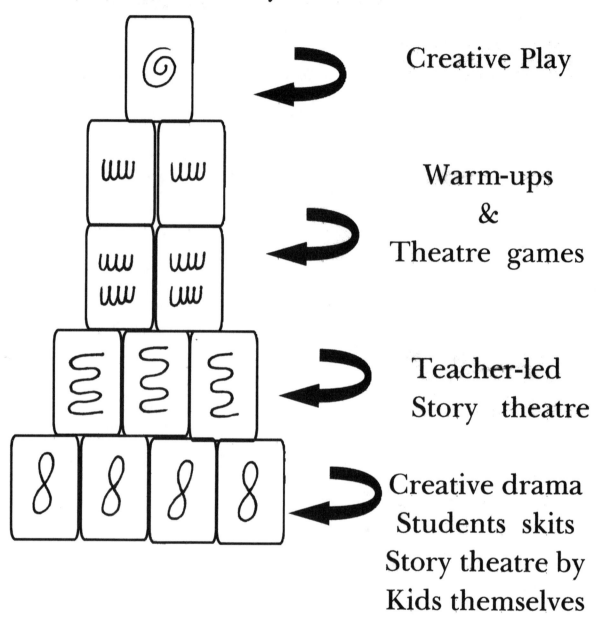

Creative Play

Warm-ups
&
Theatre games

Teacher-led
Story theatre

Creative drama
Students skits
Story theatre by
Kids themselves

Figure 6.1

Drama Pyramid Cards

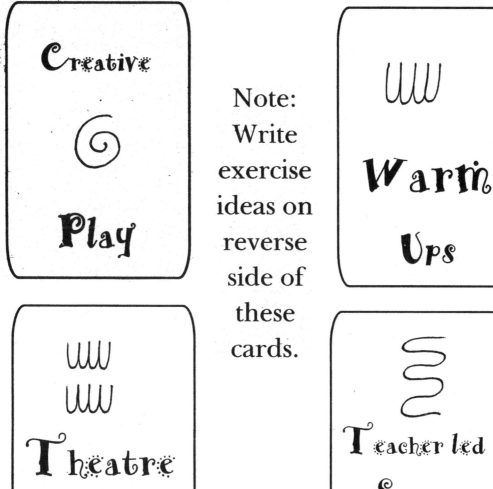

Note: Write exercise ideas on reverse side of these cards.

Warm Ups

Teacher led Story Theatre

Creative Drama, Skits, & Story Theatre by Kids Themselves

Figure 6.2

Warm-Up Cards (WUGs)

The following list of WUGs will motivate the teacher and students to begin.

- "Taking the Stage": Each student stands in front of the whole group. In turn, the student takes a self-confident pose and looks at the audience, saying nothing but simply bowing. The audience applauds as if the student actor has performed well. (Good confidence builder.)

- "Freeze, Melt": Students are instructed to move around the room like snowflakes—gently falling, dancing, whirling, and so on. Then the leader says "Freeze," and all action stops. After a minute, the leader says, "Melt" so that all frozen snowflakes can move and slowly begin to dissolve.

- "Body Seasons": Students are asked to lie down on the floor as they become the earth. With gentle guidewords, the leader tells children that they are becoming covered with a soft layer of snow. The snow increases until the earth is covered with a heavy and heavier layer of snow. Slow the action so that children begin to feel the weight of this snow. Pause for several minutes. Then tell children that winter is beginning to defrost. They may start to move fingers until they are moving their whole hands and arms. Arms rise as buds and branches start to grow. Later children may stand and let their "branches" spread and blow in the wind. (Spring and summer have arrived!) With guiding words from the leaders, students then release their leaves and begin to shrink to their knees and lie down as fall arrives. Action ends as it began with winter arriving again. Everyone lies still.

- "Clothes Become the Man or Woman" (prepare a box of clothes props ahead of time for this activity—boots, capes, hats, etc.): As each child comes forward to pull an article of clothing from the clothes box, he or she puts it on and becomes a character who "fits" the clothing. Give children some "prompts" such as, "If you choose a pair of tall boots, maybe you can walk like a giant. Show us this action." "If you choose a cape, maybe it is invisible and you can become a magical person. Are you a dragon? A wizard?"

- "In the Mood": Practice using vocal inflections by inviting children to say the phrase, "Will you hand me the mail?" Think of various kinds of mail you might be anticipating—a letter from a good friend, a report from school, a bill, an autographed picture from a rock star or sports figure, and so forth. Use angry, fearful, happy, and confused vocal inflections. Think of other phrases and emotions you might express.

Teacher-Led Story Theatre (TLSTs)

The following list of TLSTs suggests books with ideas for retelling stories with students. The teacher reads or tells the story then assigns lines or actions for students. Build on the brief suggestions given.

1. Suggested Science Books for Story Theatre

Girls Think of Everything: Stories of Ingenious Inventions by Women by Catherine Thimmesh. Houghton Mifflin, 2000.

Numerous stories about inventions are told in vivid narrative that will adapt well to story theatre activities. Mary Anderson's "Windshield Wipers" story is a winner. Engineers tackled the problem of trying to clear windshields but failed. Plucky Mary used good science thinking. She observed drivers striving to see through icy windshields, thought about how levers with arms on the outside of car windows might work, and then patented her design in 1903. Even though someone else actually manufactured the windshield wiper, Mary was a pioneer in the field. The teacher can read the story and have children take the parts of frustrated motorists, Mary, and the companies who refused her design, making up their own dialogue.

Other Good Science Books to Use for Story Theatre

Bears Out There by Joanne Ryder. Atheneum, 1995.

A boy imagines bears in the woods that play and act like he does during the course of a day. The teacher/librarian could designate children to work in twos to reenact the parts of the bear and boy as the story is read or retold. Children are encouraged to use mime to explore the resonate words in this text.

Note: Ryder's numerous books use poetic texts and close observation of nature that make them excellent sources for creative drama.

Dinosaur Detectives by Peter Chrisp. Dorling Kindersley, 2001.

This easy reader is told in a lively style with plenty of dialogue that can be easily adapted to story theatre. It includes ten stories about people who discovered fossils and bones of dinosaurs.

The Great Kapok Tree by Lynne Cherry. Harcourt Brace, 1990.

This modern classic can be easily adapted for story theatre. For specific details, refer to the chapter in this book about the rainforest.

Here Is the Tropical Rain Forest by Madeleine Dunphy. Hyperion, 1994.

Unlike the retelling of the previous book, this one is a cumulative story told in poetic text that should probably be read as it appears in the book. Children may take parts of the different plants, animals, and forces of nature to tell the story through actions and sounds so that the reading becomes an enhanced story theatre activity.

Patrick's Dinosaurs by Carol Carrick. Clarion, 1993.

Hank takes his younger brother Patrick around town, to the zoo, and home again as older brother shows off his knowledge. Patrick's wild imagination sees dinosaurs at every turn, and these fantasies are shown in the book's illustrations. The teacher/librarian can read or retell the story with children adding their own dialogue and actions so that an audience will also be able to see the two levels of this amusing story.

Stone Girl, Bone Girl: The Story of Mary Anning by Laurence Anholt. Orchard, 1999.

This lively biography of Mary Anning who discovered an ichthyosaur skeleton in 1811 can be the basis of a story theatre interpretation. The teacher/librarian may choose to use segments from Anning's entire life or create an in-depth account of her early life.

Science Resource Books to Use

Keepers of the Earth by Michael J. Caduto and Joseph Bruchac. Fulcrum, 1988.

All the "Keepers" series are excellent to combine story and science concepts.

Sharing Nature with Children by Joseph Cornell. Dawn Publications, 1988.

Sharing Nature with Children II by Joseph Cornell. Dawn Publications, 1989.

2. *Suggested Mythology and Legend Collection for Story Theatre*

Wise Women: Folk and Fairy Tales from Around the World, retold and edited by Suzanne Barchers.
Libraries Unlimited, 1990.

Many excellent brief retellings can be used for story theatre directed by a teacher or adapted by children themselves. Two of my favorite tales are the ever-popular "Molly Whuppie" from Scotland and the Native American "The Flying Head," a kind of monster tale. Because there are only two main characters in this last tale, the leader may designate many children to take the parts of other monsters and spirits living in the night.

Other Good Legends and Folktales to Use

The Leopard's Drum by Jessica Souhami. Little Brown, 1995.

The Magic Orange Tree and Other Haitian Folktales collected by Diane Wolkstein. Schocken, 1978.

Night Dancer by Marcia Vaughan. Orchard Books, 2002.

Odysseus and the Cyclops retold by Warwick Hutton. Margaret McElderry, 1995.

Note: This small sample reflects such diverse cultures as African, Haitian, Native American, and Greek. There are thousands of legends suitable to use for story theatre. Browse the 398.2 Dewey area of your public library to explore this category.

3. *Suggested History Book for Story Theatre*

Joining the Boston Tea Party by Diane Stanley. Joanna Cotler Books, HarperCollins, 2001.

This Time-Traveling Twins book lends itself beautifully to a story theatre activity. When Liz and Lenny visit their grandmother, who dons her time-travel cape, all three are transported back to Boston in 1773. They hear discontented colonists complain about British taxes, plot the famous Boston Tea Party, and take part in the action. Dialogue provided in speech balloons apart from the basic text are natural asides for student actors to use. Children may decide to create their own words to tell the story along with the leader who reads or tells the story. This book can serve as a model for writing other classroom scripts set in various periods of history.

Other Good History Books for Story Theatre

The Wall by Eve Bunting. Clarion, 1990.

This sensitive story about a boy and his father who visit the Vietnam War Memorial wall in Washington, D.C., can be adapted as story theatre with the teacher/librarian reading only the bare bones of the story. Children who take the parts of the father, the boy, and other visitors to the wall may use similar words to the characters in the book or use their own words to tell the essence of the story. Today's children will need a brief history lesson or should research the Vietnam War as this book is shared. In addition to the story theatre production, teachers may want to add an activity about grave rubbings.

Note: Eve Bunting has written numerous thoughtful books about historical events for elementary school–age children.

We Were There, Too!: Young People in U.S. History by Phillip Hoose. Farrar, Straus & Giroux, 2001.

Teachers and librarians may wish to add dialogue to the informative short biographies of the childhood of dozens of famous Americans included in this exciting text. Sidebars, photographs, and a lively narrative style contribute to this weighty volume.

Who's Stepping on Plymouth Rock? by Jean Fritz. Coward, McCann & Geoghegan, 1975.

This book may be difficult to find except in libraries, but it is well worth the effort to locate it. It tells the historical account of the controversy over preserving the "original" Plymouth Rock and can be a humorous story theatre production to adapt from Jean Fritz's excellent shorter text. The teacher/librarian may retell the entire story or select a segment to read and have children act out with their own dialogue.

Note: Jean Fritz's histories range from picture-book length to full chapter books. All are lively narratives—well researched and perfect to use in story theatre. They will motivate even the most bored student to learn more about our nation's history.

4. *Music, Dance, and Art Books for Story Theatre*

Note: Some of these may be challenging but offer tremendous opportunities for creative story theatre. More ideas are presented for this section.

Suggested Music Book

Charlie Parker Played Be Bop by Chris Raschka. Orchard, 1992.

Charlie Parker is the only human character in this book, but the figures of bopping feet, lollypops, street signs, and a black cat can be animated by children moving as these "characters." Kids may want to make large lollypop and boot stick puppets as props to move and make appropriate rhythmic sounds and movements to retell this impressionistic, jazzy story. Think of it as vocal jazz!

Other Books about the Arts to Use

Earthdance by Joanne Ryder. Holt, 1996.

This poetic text may be adapted as story theatre or used in a creative dramatic exercise. As story theatre children can take the parts of children from different parts of the world, as forces in nature (wind, clouds, oceans, sun), and animals to move and join in one joyous earthdance. Ryder's books begin with close observation of nature then stretch children's imaginations through poetic texts.

Katie and the Sunflowers by James Mayhew. Orchard Books, 2000.

A little girl goes to the art museum with her grandmother on a rainy day and literally steps into some of the famous paintings. This inventive story will delight children as the teacher guides students to pose as if they were in a painting and then "step" through a mimed picture frame (children take parts as the picture frame). Instruct children to create actions as the children do in this story.

Creative Drama and Student Story Theatre/Skits (CDSTs)

The following list of CDST's (Creative Drama and Student Story Theatre/Skits) can be used if the teacher or school librarian chooses to extend this unit into a longer time frame. It might also be used as an after school activity for a drama club.

1. Skits are brief summaries of story plots for characters to develop on their own. These skits, coauthored with Robin Currie, were published in our book *Straw into Gold* (Libraries Unlimited, 1993.) The two included here are based on popular folktales and can be performed by kids with their own dialogue and actions.

2. *Amazing Grace* by Mary Hoffman (Dial, 1991) is one of the best examples of a story that lends itself to creative dramatic activities. The Minneapolis Children's Theatre's production of this story used the book's storyline then presented vignettes that seemed to grow spontaneously from the sparse words and illustrations in Hoffman's book. Read the book to children and guide them as they develop their own scenes based on some of the details in the story. For example, explore Anansi stories for children to retell. Find a brief retelling of Aladdin and his lamp for children to develop as creative dramatics. Read "Puss and Boots" and help children retell the story with mime and actions.

3. Choose several versions of the folktale "Jack and the Beanstalk" and help children tell their own version. Encourage them to think of people taking the parts of inanimate objects such as the beanstalk. With guidance, kids will make interesting choices. In one library where I have worked, about ten children decided to become a living beanstalk, but rather than standing on top of one another's shoulders (a risky venture), they decided to lay on the floor as the Jack character walked around them on his way to the giant and back to earth.

Watch Your Time

Characters: Sidney, magical person, royal person, assorted animals, people at the ball

Plot: Sidney (a boy or girl) is left alone when everyone else goes to the ball. A magic person (male or female) promises to help, but the magic is a little off base. Instead of changing white mice into horses, they turn into camels. Other problems happens (develop these on your own), but Sidney is finally off to the ball. Sidney meets the royal person but loses track of time. She/he is transformed back into rags at the ball. The royal person tries to help Sidney dress up again, but no one is too concerned with appearances. The wedding occurs right on the spot.

Don't Go In!

Characters: Papa Bear, Mama Bear, Baby Bear, Goldilocks, trees in forest (as many as you like), many forest animals

Plot: The Bears leave their breakfast on the table and go for a walk. Goldilocks comes through the woods. Trees and animals warn her not to go into the forest, certainly not to the Bears' house. She does anyway, eats the breakfast, sits in the chairs, tries the beds, and goes to sleep. Back in the forest, the trees and animals tell the Bears to return home. They do and find Goldie asleep in Baby Bear's bed. Goldie is apologetic, and this time the Bears forgive her as she promises to stay to clean up and never return again.

A Day to Act Out: A Creative Dramatics Program for Public Libraries

Public libraries often incorporate a creative dramatics activity within other programs or storytimes for younger children. This program devotes a full program to creative dramatics for school-age children. Librarians in youth departments usually do these programs themselves, but some staff like to involve teachers or high school drama students and teachers as consultants.

The following program presents different options to choose.

Materials Needed

1. Scripts, if needed, for story theatre

2. Prop boxes for children to select props or simple costumes as creative play begins

3. Paper, markers, poster board, scissors, tape, glue, etc. if students are expected to construct their own props

Procedure

1. Welcome participants to join the "Library's Acting Out" Group for the Day.

2. Establish "ground rules" (based on the Tip Sheet provided in this chapter) so that everyone will have a positive experience with guidelines that promote respect and cooperation.

3. Use one or two warm-up games (as listed in the Drama Pyramid) or find others based on books in the bibliography.

4. Divide the large group into several smaller drama troupes so that children will be able to participate in guided activities. A rule of thumb is that six to ten children usually make up a good-sized group. Involving twenty to thirty children in the same story can result in chaos and a less than satisfactory experience for everyone. If the library does not have enough staff members for three or four people to help, enlist the assistance of parents, teachers, or college students. Be careful about expecting high school students to take on this role alone. In my experience, teens are usually not mature enough to take charge of children just a few years younger than they are. Trained high school drama students can be great assistants but often need the authority of an adult to direct the energies of children.

5. Try to find separate "practice spaces" for each group if you can. A large room may be divided into separate spaces depending on acoustics, but several smaller areas are better. Have each creative dramatics or story theatre group practice for about thirty minutes with a leader. Choose one of the stories in the Drama Pyramid, or create dinosaur stories using ideas in this chapter. Invite all children back to the "Acting It Out" Space. Do another warm-up game to bring the full group together in a spirit of camaraderie. Perhaps children will enjoy playing "Name That Dinosaur" as described later.

6. Have each group introduce their drama activity or story theatre script to perform for the group as a whole. Before this "production" takes place, ask all children to take another part, that of audience players. Audience players listen, look, and clap in the same way that they would like the audience to treat them. Children today will need this kind of reminder because thoughtful audience behavior is not as prevalent as it was in the past.

7. End the Day of Acting Out with simple recognition, such as certificates for performance, juice, popcorn or crackers and cheese, and handshakes and pats on the back for good jobs well done.

Dinosaur Drama

Because the topic of dinosaurs is an ever-popular subject for many children, the following three creative dramatics activities should work with a wide age range of children attending a school-age program at the public library. The book *Dinosaur Detectives* by Peter Chrisp is an important reference for all three groups, and thus the librarian in charge may wish to purchase several copies of the book. Other excellent dinosaur books will work if you wish to create different creative dramatics dinosaur activities. The dinosaur script found in the appendix of this book could also be used.

If you want to serve "dinosaur treats," you can look for dinosaur-shaped cereal, crackers, or cookies. Or ask volunteers to make bone-shaped cookies from refrigerated rolls of sugar cookies that can be quickly rolled out and cut into bone shapes.

Group I: Fossil Woman

Tell the story of Mary Anning, born in 1799 in Lyme Regis, England. The daughter of a carpenter, her father took her to the beach on Sundays to look for fossils. Using the Anholt or Chrisp books (or both) listed in the Drama Pyramid, create dialogue between Mary and her father as she looks for fossils, or re-create the story of Mary and her brother discovering the sea horse fossils and showing them to excited visitors. This second option will give more children a chance to participate.

Group II: Big Tooth

Using the Chrisp book about Gideon Mantell, retell the story of Gideon and his wife Mary Ann when the young wife discovers a dinosaur tooth. Include parts of the workmen (and women even though there may not actually have been women workers then) so that more children can participate.

Group III: Dinner in a Dinosaur

Retell the bizarre story (found in the Chrisp book) about the scientists who ate dinner inside the model of a giant Iguanodon. Except for Host Richard Owen, you will need to make up names for the other party guests and create dialogue. (Think what you might say if you were invited to such a party!)

Name That Dinosaur

Play this game in the manner of "I Unpacked Grandmother's Trunk." In this game, seat children in a circle. One child begins by saying "I unpacked Grandmother's trunk, and I found an . . . (alligator or some other object beginning with an A). The next child repeats what child one has said then adds another object, this one beginning with the letter B.

For the dinosaur version, the first child says, "I went on a dinosaur dig and I found an . . . (allosaur)." The next child will repeat allosaur then think of a dinosaur beginning with a B letter. (I would allow the name "brontosaurus" even though recent sources rename that dinosaur "apatosaurus.") If no one can think of a dinosaur for some letters of the alphabet, just skip that letter and call out the next letter in alphabetical order.

Fantasy Worlds

My son has been a juggler since he was a child. He used to pick up fruits and vegetables in the grocery, and, much to my dismay, he juggled them. I pleaded with him to stop, but he was a persistent child. He continued to juggle oranges, apples, bananas, and even peppers. I suppose it was my fault though, in the first place, because I read Tomie dePaola's *Clown of God* to him many times. We both were caught up in the magic of the juggler's feat—throwing up a rainbow of colored balls and keeping them suspended in midair. Lacking hand-to-eye coordination, I cannot physically juggle, but in my mind's eye, I continue to toss up paradoxical ideas and wonder how we live in a world with such contradictions.

Perhaps you too have wondered why young people stick cell phones to their ears as they walk down shopping malls surrounded by their friends. Are they afraid they aren't connected enough? Why do kids who amass video libraries of their own, towers of electronic games, sophisticated audio systems squeezed into boxes the size of a pack of cards then complain that they are bored? Why in a world with war, drugs, suicide, and all manner of disagreements do children today hunger for books filled with old-fashioned dragons, wizards, and mice that fall in love with princesses?

Do you ever wonder about things like this? Escape seeking may be a partial answer for the flood of fantasy books young people can't seem to get enough of. But why does fantasy seem so particularly important to kids today? What books in this popular genre might we select for a basic library collection? And what kinds of related programs and activities can librarians provide that will make a difference to the kids who look to fantasy literature in a complex and confusing time?

T. A. Barron, in his article "The Remarkable Metaphor of Merlin" (*Book Links,* January 1998), suggests that the revival of interest in the wizard and his lore at the close of the second millennium may be because we are looking for someone who can "bring us together, who can cross any boundaries." Jane Yolen in *Touch Magic* tells us that a child who loves "the oddities of a fantasy book cannot possibly be xenophobic as an adult." (I'd love to chisel that on the walls of schools and libraries to remind well-meaning parents wishing to protect children. Please do not take fantasy books away from your children if you want them to grow up strong and able to face their fears!) Consider the message behind Lemony Snickett's books. Children may find themselves in desperate circumstances, but if they stick together and use their wits, they dramatically increase their chances to survive most unimaginably terrible situations. Finally, the most inspiring remark I found is the note at the beginning of *The Tale of Despereaux,* the 2004 Newbery Award–winning book. Kate DiCamillo gently says, "The world is dark, and the light is precious. Come closer, dear reader. You must trust me. I am telling you a story."

Fantasy literature has its roots in a long tradition of legend and traditional literature. Most of the memorable classics such as *Alice in Wonderland, the Wizard of Oz, Wind in Willows, Winnie-the-Pooh, Charlotte's Web,* and *The Lion, the Witch, and the Wardrobe,* fall into this genre. These stories deal with universal themes that are timeless and appealing to children from one generation to the next. The topic is immense, and, certainly just one chapter in this book cannot pretend to be comprehensive.

The bibliography of this chapter must be highly selective. Books from the different subdivisions of fantasy—animal or beast tales, allegorical tales, fantasy set in other worlds, quest tales, time-travel stories, toy fantasy, wish and witch or dragon tales are listed. Some titles are classics, and others are contemporary. A few newer series books are represented, but because of the overwhelming number of these being published, the focus is on only a few so that I could include many individual titles. There is a balance of books to interest both male and female readers. Short and longer titles appear. Fantasy books are overwhelmingly popular with young adults, but *Stories, Time and Again* spans the elementary-age group only. I asked children's librarians to send their favorite fantasy titles to me for this book, and these lists appear in the Appendix. This bibliography is a not meant to be a "core collection" tool. It is one of many lists.

A variety of program activities from a Fantasy Tree Trivia Game and a wall mural to writing book blurbs and original fantasies are given for planning programs in public and school libraries. Some of these are reminiscent of the folk literature exercises and the ideas in the creative dramatics chapter. You may wish to use some activities interchangeably as appropriate.

Finally, there is a great omission for obvious reasons. None of the Harry Potter books are mentioned nor are any Harry Potter programs presented. (This may be as serious as teaching the alphabet without mentioning the vowels.) Certainly, J. K. Rowling's contribution to fantasy literature and the popularity of her books has changed all of our lives. Her characters are well drawn; the themes, universal; the style, distinctive; and the storytelling, compelling. Perhaps no other living children's author has inspired more children to read than Rowling. Even the *New York Times* Book Review began listing children's best sellers on a separate list due to the popularity of the Harry Potter books. But the Harry Potter books are for another project, and so this chapter is about other fantasies children will want to read when they have finished reading about Harry and are waiting for the next Rowling book to appear on library bookshelves.

Bibliography

Alexander, Lloyd. *The Book of Three*. Holt, 1964.
    Based on Welsh folk literature, Alexander's high fantasy tale about Taran's quest to become a hero is the first of the Chronicles of Prydain. Other titles include *The Black Cauldron, The Castle of Llyr, The High King,* and *Taran Wanderer.*

Baum, L. Frank. *The Wizard of Oz*. Illustrated by Lisbeth Zwerger. North South, 1996.
    In this first of Baum's fantasies about the Land of Oz, Dorothy meets a scarecrow, tin woodsman, and a lion who accompany her on adventures in a fairy-tale land to find the great wizard. This newly illustrated edition by watercolor artist Lisbeth Zwerger presents very different images of these well-known characters.

Bellairs, John. *The House with a Clock in Its Walls*. Puffin, 1993 (originally published in 1973).
    Lewis goes to live with his Uncle Jonathan in an old house with secret passageways and soon discovers that his uncle is a wizard and the house has a clock in the walls. The clock is marking off time until the end of the world.

Brittain, Bill. *The Wish Giver*. Harper, 1983.
    In this tale of Coven Tree, various people receive cards from Thaddeus Blinn, who grants wishes. The catch is that people make foolish wishes and end up with exactly what they have wished for. The side effects are horrible and amusing. Other title: *Dr. Dredd's Wagon of Wonders.*

Carle, Eric. *Draw Me a Star*. Penguin Putnam, 1992.
    When an artist draws a star, all things on Earth and in the sky beckon the artist to draw for them too. Carle's bold fantasy drawings and the simple but profound story invite children to be artists and create their own stars. This book can serve as springboard for the topic of fantasy and of using one's imagination.

Cleary, Beverly. *The Mouse and the Motorcycle*. William Morrow, 1965.

In this first fantasy of three, a boy meets Ralph, the mouse, who motors around in the boy's toy motorcycle. The story is set firmly in a real world, but the fantasy exchange between boy and mouse seems perfectly natural. Other titles: *Runaway Ralph, Ralph S. Mouse.*

Cooper, Susan. *Over Sea, Under Stone*. Harcourt, 1965.

Three children discover an old map in a house in Cornwall and end up searching for the Holy Grail in this first of the high fantasy books capturing the spirit of an Arthurian quest. Other titles: *The Dark Is Rising, Greenwitch, The Grey King,* and *Silver on the Tree.*

Dahl, Roald. *James and the Giant Peach*. Illustrated by Lane Smith. Alfred A. Knopf, 1996.

When James becomes orphaned, he is sent to live with his awful Aunt Sponge and Aunt Spiker. Life improves, however, when an old man gives him magic crystals that turn a peach into an enchanted place where James enjoys the company of joyful creatures. Smith's quirky black-and-white pen drawings add to this popular fantasy.

Dicamillo, Kate. *The Tale of Despereaux*. Candlewick, 2003.

In this Newbery Award book, a small, talented mouse, a rat who loves light, a princess, and a girl who wishes to be a princess embark on adventures that bring the unlikely set of characters together in a gentle fantasy.

Eager, Edward. *Half Magic*. Harcourt Brace, 1999 (originally published in 1954).

Four children discover a coin that is magic but only "half magic," so the results are only half invisible, half rescued—half everything. The light-hearted fantasy is a good bridge book between longer picture books and more complex fantasy novels. Other title: *Well Wishers.*

Ibbotson, Eva. *The Secret of Platform 13*. Dutton, 1998 (originally published in 1994).

A hag, a wizard, a fey, and an ogre travel from their magical island to London to rescue the king's son. Some parallels with the Harry Potter books will add to this book's appeal for fantasy loving kids. Other title: *The Haunting of Granite Falls.*

Le Guin, Ursula K. *Wonderful Alexander and the Catwings*. Orchard Books, 1994.

Alexander Furball, the strongest kitten in the family, is treed by two barking hounds, but a winged cat rescues him. Alexander goes on to help a winged cat that doesn't talk like the rest of her family. Other titles for older readers: *A Wizard of Earthsea, Tombs of Atun,* and *Farthest Shore.*

McLachlan, Patricia. *Tomorrow's Wizard*. Harper & Row, 1982.

Murdoch and his mentor, Tomorrow's Wizard, make wishes come true for several people in surprising ways. This shorter novel makes a good read aloud in a school setting, and is a good choice for children before they tackle more complex fantasies.

Milne, A. A. *Winnie-the-Pooh*. Dutton, 1926.

Perhaps the most beloved bear in the world, Pooh and his animal friends take Christopher Robin with them on many wonderful adventures in One Hundred Acre Wood. Other title: *The House at Pooh Corner.*

Nimmo, Jenny. *Midnight for Charlie Bone*. Orchard, 2002

Charlie discovers he has unusual gifts such as being able to look at photographs and hear the conversations that were taking place when the photos were taken. When the boy goes to attend Bloor's Academy, he becomes involved in dangerous intrigues. This book has parallels with the Harry Potter books.

Norton, Mary. *The Borrowers*. Harcourt, 2003 (originally published in 1986).

The little people—Pod, Homily, and Arriety—secretly live under the floorboards of a house and take things from the people who live in the house. Other title: *The Borrowers Afloat.*

Pearce, Philippa. *Tom's Midnight Garden*. Lippincott, 1959.

Tom is shipped off to live with an aunt and uncle in the country when he brother gets sick. At first he is displeased, but when he discovers a magical garden and meets a new friend, he wishes he could stay with his relatives forever.

Reynolds, Peter H. *Ish*. Candlewick, 2004.

Ramon loves to draw but becomes frustrated when his drawings don't look exactly right. His sister, Marisol, resurrects his crumpled drawings and shows him that his drawings have significant "ish" qualities as in "tree-ish," "house-ish." This story celebrates creativity and finding one's own voice, important components in reading and understanding fantasy literature.

Reynolds, Peter H. *Sydney's Star*. Simon & Schuster, 2001

A young mouse inventor decides to make a star with a remote control, but it malfunctions as she is showing it at the student science fair. As Sydney is bemoaning her loss, the star comes back to her along with a sea captain who was guided out of a storm by the amazing star. This picture book can inspire discussions about creativity, using the imagination, and believing in one's own special talents.

Snicket, Lemony. *The Bad Beginning*. HarperCollins, 1999.

Three children learn their parents have died and must live with the awful Count Olaf. This story and its sequels (*The Reptile Room, The Wide Window*, et al.) present one terrible situation after another, but the children prevail because of their talents, bravery, and commitment to one another. This is part of the popular "A Series of Unfortunate Events."

Steig, William. *Sylvester and the Magic Pebble*. Windmill, 1969.

A donkey makes a wish with a magic pebble, with unfortunate results.

Van Allsburg, Chris. *Jumanji*. Houghton Mifflin, 1981.

Two children find a board game in the park, and when they take it home, it comes alive, taking them on jungle adventures they never dreamed could happen. Other title: *The Polar Express.*

White, E. B. *Charlotte's Web*. Harper, 1952.

Charlotte the spider saves Wilbur the pig's life when she weaves messages into her webs, thus proving to a farmer and the whole community that this is no ordinary pig. The animal fantasy works beautifully alongside the down-to-earth story.

Winthrop, Elizabeth. *The Castle in the Attic*. Holiday, 1985.

A boy receives a real-looking castle, and when he picks up a tiny knight, it comes alive!

Yolen, Jane. *The Dragon's Boy: A Tale of Young King Arthur*. Harper, 2001.

This tale of an orphan raised by Sir Ector sets out on a remarkable destiny. Most of Yolen's fantasies are for an older audience, but upper elementary students will enjoy this one.

"Open Doors Just Beyond": A Fantasy Program for School Libraries

This program will introduce students to an overview of fantasy literature. Both classic and contemporary books, some picture books and longer fiction are included in the activities. Using the read-aloud suggestions, the writing and speaking exercises, and the "book blurb" activity, educators will help kids improve their language and literacy skills and motivate children to read broadly from this favorite genre.

Materials Needed

1. Several rolls of brown wrapping paper or large sheets of art paper for wall mural

2. Paints, large markers, scissors, and glue for mural

3. Colored paper for Fantasy Tree

Procedure

1. In preparation for this program, make a fantasy wall mural using ideas from the Fantasy Wall Mural Page in this chapter.

2. The teacher/librarian introduces the topic of fantasy by reading one or more of the following picture books: *Draw Me a Star* by Eric Carle, *Sydney's Star* by Peter H. Reynolds, or *Ish* by Peter H. Reynolds. Follow the readings with a lively discussion about using the imagination. Read the poem "Wishingly on a Star." Ask students to write a brief response to the poem. The response might begin, "The part of this poem that best describes an experience I have had is . . . ."

3. Students select a fantasy book to read for this unit from a display of books the librarian selects. Use the bibliography in this chapter and consult some of the lists appearing in the appendix for your display.

4. The teacher/librarian reads a short fantasy book such as *Tomorrow's Wizard* by Patricia MacLachlan or *Wonderful Alexander and the Catwings* by Ursula K. Le Guin. Students continue reading the fantasy books they selected during the previous session. Librarian describes the "book blurb" process so that students will be able to tell one another succinctly about the book they are reading. Allow time for students to write their book blurbs at the end of this session.

5. Students share their book blurbs. The librarian prompts kids to choose ideas from the Fantasy Tree in writing their own short fantasies. The fantasies may be turned in later, and a scrapbook of these can be kept in the school library.

Wishingly on Stars

Are you a someone who stops to wish on stars
Or dares to look down
From high rooftops?
Have you looked up
Caught a falling star
In the corner of your eye,
And thought
I wish I might go out there
Just somewhere . . .
Did you ever fall asleep
And wake up
On the other side of
Tomorrow?
Did you ever keep a secret
Because you thought
No one would believe
The dream you had last night
Was too good to be true?
If you have ever thought—
Just for one moment—
Things like this
May be
Possible,
You know
That's how
Unimaginable
Things You Imagine
Will
Very likely
Happen
If you continue to think
Wishingly on
Stars.

—Jan Irving Duncan-O'Neal

Fantasy Wall Mural

Students with artistic talents may be enlisted to help create this wall mural. Attach large art paper or brown wrapping paper to the wall for students to add abstract designs or paint with large brush strokes of color for a background to the collage. Intriguing photos of anything—animals, outer space, dreamlike images, eyes, hands, footprints—will fill the background.

Intersperse these images with quotes and thoughts about fantasy. The chart below titled "Fantasy Is . . ." will give children a guide for understanding the elements of fantasy. Other quotes could lead into class discussion.

Fantasy Quotes and Quips

- "Imaginary gardens with real toads in them. . . " —Marianne Moore
- "Fantasy defines the universe." —Ruth Nadelman Lynn
- "Fantasy novels are waking dreams." —Jane Langton
- "A fantasy is a journey . . . it can change you." —Ursula Le Guin
- "[Fantasy is] the most magnificent bubble I have ever seen . . . achingly beautiful." —Susan Cooper
- "It is not an escape, not an entertainment. . . . It is not an escape from life. It is a coming to terms with reality." —Alan Garner
- Fantasy makes the impossible, possible!
- Fantasy readers do not give up on life. They believe in the kind of hope that things really will work out in the end!
- Fads come and go. Fantasy stays with us like a wise old person or our most deeply held beliefs.

Fantasy Is . . .

- rooted in traditional myths and legends.
- full of important themes.
- challenging—it challenges readers to open themselves up to believing strange or unbelievable things can happen.
- an unreal world—it may begin in the real world but then moves into a secondary unreal world.
- a special, unique setting.
- a story with characters and action like all fiction but does not happen in the "real world."
- an animal tale with talking beasts or a story with toys that come alive, a world of little people, or a supernatural story.
- a quest story of great adventure when the main character searches for something of value such as a grail or magic goblet.
- a story for people who can think beyond the ordinary, everyday.
- a story that confronts large issues such as the battle between good and evil.

Book Blurbs

Book blurbs, by my definition, are little nuggets of information or tantalizing tidbits about a book that inspire someone to read a book. They are not as comprehensively concise as a book annotation that is written by a person at the Library of Congress and printed on the reverse side of the title page of a book. (This information is part of the CIP or "Cataloging in Publication" data that informs the reader about the basic nature of a book.)

Book blurbs may be the phrases a publisher uses on the back cover of a book or on the dust jacket. In a sense, blurbs are little "advertisements." They are "hooks" to capture a potential reader.

Book blurbs are not dull. They do not rely on such lifeless phrases as "This book is great . . . or interesting . . . or colorful . . . or wonderful."

Book blurbs help students get past the habit of rambling on and on about a book. Too often when asked to tell about a book he is reading, a boy might ramble on and on and what happens in the story. A girl might become so excited to tell about a book that she tries to tell the whole story. I have found that too many book discussion groups in libraries result in kids boring other kids instead of exciting one another about the books they are reading.

Book blurbs are a kind of "springboard" or a first step into learning to write book summaries or annotations. They can be terrific opportunities to encourage kids to focus their thinking and speak briefly in an effective way.

In helping students write book blurbs, the librarian might say something like this:

> Keep your book blurb short, not more than three or four sentences. This doesn't give you enough time to actually tell the whole story, or even very much about it. Think to yourself, *What if I only had one minute to tell my best friend something about this book that would guarantee he (or she) would pick it up immediately?* This kind of quick, to the point, focus on a book's appeal is just what you want to do.

> To write a good book blurb, think of *specific,* descriptive words about the book or your response to it. Here is a sample book blurb for *The Secret of Platform 13* by Eva Ibbotson. "Platform 13 may not be a place you dare to go to. It is rusty and rundown and has a secret door." This book blurb for *Jennifer Murdley's Toad* tells something of the beginning action, but it doesn't tell us very much. "In this book, a girl runs away from kids who are teasing her. She goes into a strange magic shop that sells unusual animals—toads, lizards, bats. She begins to think something special will happen to her."

Fantasy Tree for Writing Your Own Fantasy

Prepare four kinds of fantasy playing cards. Choose a different color of copier paper for each kind of card to distinguish the categories—Character, Setting, Action, Magic Objects, or Helpmates. Each individual card will be the size of half a piece of 8 1/2 x 11–inch copy paper. These colored cards will be attached to branches of the fantasy tree described in the program "Wonderfully Fantastic." Children choose one card from each category to inspire them in writing original fantasies either in small groups or as individuals. Each group or individual will need a set of four cards. Duplicate cards for each category can be written, but to make this activity interesting, I suggest writing a variety.

The following cards will serve as examples. You will want to create additional cards of your own.

Character Card

Four girls your own age who are interested in sports. Name them and write a brief description of each girl.

Character Card

A sister and a brother who don't always get along but will stick together in difficult situations. Name the kids and describe them briefly.

Character Card

A boy and his best friend: they have opposite skills that will prove useful when they are faced with problems. Name the kids and describe these skills.

Setting Card

Primary World—A small town in a resort area in someplace in the United States. (Describe this place where the adventure begins.)

Secondary/Imaginary World—Underground habitat where magic people live. (Describe this place and the magic people.)

Setting Card

Primary World—The suburb of a large city during the summer when the kids are home from school. (Describe the place more specifically.)

Secondary World—A place where small forest people live inside trees, in caves, and under mushrooms. (Describe the place and these small people.)

Setting Card

Primary World—A school gymnasium after school. (Describe this place where the adventure begins.)

Secondary World—Another planet in the universe inhabited by a highly intelligent species of people. (Describe this planet and the people.)

Action Card

The characters go to the secondary world because someone in this magical place visits them in the "real world." The characters do not want to take this journey, but they are forced to go anyway. In the secondary world, the characters must solve three problems to find their way home. (Describe these journeys and the three problems. Show how the characters solve these problems.)

Action Card

The characters in the story receive a letter telling them to go to a special place where they will be taken by a magic vehicle to the secondary world. The characters are afraid to go, but they talk themselves into it. The secondary world proves to be very exciting, but the characters tire of too much excitement. They find the magic vehicle and return home just in time for dinner. (Write the letter, describe the vehicle and the exciting action.)

Action Card

One of the characters has a dream that transports all the characters into the secondary world. The characters find themselves on a quest to find a valuable object to take home to bring about a peaceful solution to some problem in the real world. (Describe the dream, the quest, the problems the characters encounter in the secondary world to receive this valuable object and how it will solve the problem back home.)

Magic Object/Helpmate Card

A magic ring grants a wish that will solve the problem. (Describe the object and how it helps the characters in their own dilemma.)

Magic Object/Helpmate Card

A kind wizard helps the characters when they prove to him that they are worthy. He is not able to solve their problem entirely but offers momentary aid. (Describe what the characters do to show their worth and what the wizard can do to help them.)

Magic Object/Helpmate Card

A magical beast or person helps the characters in three ways, but the characters must do three things to reward the beast so that it will agree to help them. (Describe this beast, what it does, and the action our characters must do to carry out the reward.)

The Ending

All groups participating in this activity need to solve the problems and complete action in a satisfying way. The characters will return to their primary world. The ending should be final and satisfying in some way.

Wonderfully Fantastic! A Fantasy Party Program for Public Libraries

Note: Because fantasy literature is written for all ages and very young children enter easily into the world of fantasy, you will need to decide whether to advertise your program for a certain age group. If you decide to open the event to all ages, you may find some of the activities described here as too difficult for preschool-age children.

This is a program for school-age children with many of the books listed for children in Grades 2 or 3 and above. Select from the activities to design a program for your own situation.

Materials Needed

1. Christmas lights, purple fabric swag

2. Coat tree or artificial Christmas tree

3. Colored paper strips, ribbons for the Fantasy Tree

4. Food for snacks (punch or ginger ale and lime sherbet, cookies)

5. Small prizes

Procedure

1. In preparation for this event, make a magical setting for the program room. Create a fanciful mood with simple props. Hang small white Christmas lights around the room and darken the main room lights for the beginning of the program.

    Swag a purple length of material across the door to the program room or tape silver paper to the door. Fill the room with clear or iridescent balloons and tape silver or glow-in-the-dark stars to the ceiling.

    Make a Fantasy Tree by hanging colored strips of paper from an artificial Christmas tree or a coat rack. On the strips of paper, write out the summaries of popular fantasy books. Children will use this Fantasy Tree when they play the Fantasy Tree Trivia Game during the program. This prop is not absolutely necessary, but it adds to the fun of the fantasy theme.

2. The librarian begins by using the guided imagery exercise provided.

3. Begin a storytelling circle with children seated in a large circle or several story circles if your group is larger than fifteen kids. Use one of the magical story starters listed later. After the leader reads the starter, she or he rings a bell indicating that the next child continues the story. Allow the second child to continue telling the story for three or four minutes, then ring the bell again for the next child to continue. If a child hesitates or does not wish to participate, the leader may suggest a direction for the story to go or simply let that child decide to gather his or her thoughts and speak later.

4. Play the Fantasy Tree Trivia Game by dividing the group into two groups. The leader reads aloud one of the summaries of fantasy books from the fantasy slips on the fantasy tree. If no fantasy tree has been made, the questions may simply be written on index cards with the title of the book and author on the reverse side of the card. Summaries and answers are provided later in this chapter.

5. Serve ginger ale with lime sherbet for a fancy beverage and sugar cookies cut in moon and star shapes for treats.

6. Encourage children to check out one of the fantasy books on a book cart on which copies of all books mentioned in the program are displayed.

Into a Fantasy Dream: A Guided Imagery Exercise

The leader reads the following script after she encourages children to sit on the floor with sufficient space between one another so everyone has a "personal dream space." Children should keep eyes shut during this activity. To add to the effectiveness of a guided imagery exercise, darken room lights so the Christmas lights are the only room illumination.

Script

As you close your eyes, imagine that you are falling slowly and silently asleep. The darkness of this room becomes a soft yellow in your dream. Imagine that this is the first light of day in a land where strange things begin to happen.

You may wish to slowly lift your arms just above your head. You can feel a warm, soft, puffy substance above your head. This is a sun cloud. It will give you a sense of wonder. Slowly, very slowly, stand up to feel the warmth of the sun cloud above your head.

Snow begins to fall on your head, but it is not cold or wet. The sun cloud protects you from the snow. In your mind, imagine that each flake is huge, almost the size of a beach ball. Yes! The snowflakes are soft and round and lightweight. They float in the air around you. Gently touch the one coming near your nose. Oh! It popped. The air smells like lemon drop candy. Breathe in deeply. You feel calm and relaxed. Lower your arms so they are slightly loose and relaxed, too.

Without moving beyond your place, tip toe in place. Imagine that you are walking down a path in a forest. The sun disappears as you move farther and farther into the forest. Stop moving. Just ahead of you lies a bridge. It is narrow and covered in deep green moss and vines. It is very old, so you will need to move carefully to go across.

Do not move but imagine you are walking across the bridge. Now, sit down on the floor. As you sit, imagine you have reached the other side of the bridge. Several roads stretch out before you. One is overgrown with brambles and thorny bushes. Another road oozes mud and slime. A third road leads deeper into the forest.

Imagine that you are moving into the forest. Above you are owls and tall trees. You move deeper into the forest, walking for a long time. Just when you think you can walk no longer, you see an enormous stone house that looks like a castle. The castle has two tall towers, ten chimneys, long narrow windows, and a large wooden door.

Carefully you walk up to that door and pull the doorknob as hard as you can to go inside. Inside everything is too dark to see objects, but as your eyes become accustomed to the dark, you make out the entrance to a long hall. In your mind's eye, walk down that hall. Stop at the room you come to at the end of the hall. There is another door. Should you open it?

What will be standing behind the door? The castle ghost? A midnight black cat? A very old wizard? You feel a bit anxious, even fearful, but you bravely push the door open, and step out into . . .

Outer space! You are floating in the Milky Way. Fragments of stars fly past you. They smell delicious. One small star sliver smells like cheese. You reach out to take it in your hand and take a bite when you suddenly wake up.

You see a plate of cheese sandwiches in front of you.

(Room lights are turned on and children are served small cheese sandwiches before the program continues. To add a fantasy touch to this treat, make open-face sandwiches from wheat or firm white bread with crusts removed. Cut bread in small squares and add a piece of cheese cut with a star-shaped cookie cutter to the top of the bread.)

Magic Story Circle Activity

Stones arranged in a circle, a ring of mushrooms growing in the forest, and a circle of dancers all appear in many fantasy stories. Remind children that a circle reminds us of never-ending ideas. The phrase "As long as there are those who listen, stories will always be told and retold. This is the power of the never-ending story." This is the reason you instruct children to sit in a circle. In the middle of the circle, place a black cauldron, purchased from a discount or toy store or one stored away with your Halloween props. From this cauldron, you take out a slice of paper on which you have written a story starter. You read this aloud to begin the story that the children will continue.

Notice that most of these story starters are inspired by famous children's books such as *Tom's Midnight Garden* and *Alice in Wonderland*. Consult other fantasy books in your library collection to write other story starters.

Proceed with this activity according to the directions given in the procedures to this program.

Story Starters

1. Tom walked into his grandfather's library. The tall clock in the corner chimes 1-2-3-4-5-6-7-8-9-10-11-12- and 13! Everything in the room changes. . . .

2. Alice touched the bathroom mirror with her toothbrush, and it disappeared.

3. Alex heard his cat say in a loud whisper, "Watch Out!"

4. Emma took a bite of a shortbread cookie and began to chew. When she swallowed the cookie, she realized she had shrunk to the size of a small mouse.

5. James jumped onto his bicycle, and the minute he touched the seat, the bicycle turned into a green dragon.

Fantasy Tree Trivia Game

A small artificial Christmas tree or a coat rack can create instant Fantasy Trees. Hang plenty of colored ribbons cut in yard long lengths from the branches to make your tree fanciful. From these ribbons attach colored strips of paper with small clothespins or colored paper clips. Write book summaries of fantasy books on these slips along with the answer with the title of the book and its author.

This game may be played in teams with one person answering the question from each team as the turns are taken. An alternative method of play would allow all team members to consult before an answer is given.

If you believe children expect a prize at the end of the game, provide prizes, such as glittery pencils or stickers, for everyone.

1. In this story, a poor young man is sent away from home to learn magic. He is given the name "Thornmallow" because he is "prickly on the outside, squishy within."

     Answer: *Wizard Hall* by Jane Yolen

2. The children in this book go to a fantasy kingdom where they receive a treat called "Turkish Delight."

     Answer: *The Lion, the Witch, and the Wardrobe* by C. S. Lewis

3. Four children are looking for an adventure. The oldest child finds a coin that she thinks is a nickel, but it is a magic coin. The coin takes the children on magical adventures.

     Answer: *Half Magic* by Edward Eager

4. A spider spins a web that reads "Some Pig."

     Answer: *Charlotte's Web* by E. B. White

5. A boy is sent out on a quest throughout the kingdom to find out what people think is delicious.

     Answer: *The Search for Delicious* by Natalie Babbitt

6. A young man goes into a garden where only a girl can see him. A grandfather's clock is an important part of this story.

     Answer: *Tom's Midnight Garden* by Philippa Pearce

7. A forgotten door on an abandoned railway station platform is the entrance to a magical kingdom with wonderful creatures.

     Answer: *The Secret of Platform 13* by Eva Ibbotson

8. When a girl checks out a red book from the library, the librarian tells her that it is a "seven-day book."

     Answer: *Seven-Day Magic* by Edward Eager

9. A boy receives a wooden model of a castle, and when he picks up a small silver knight from the castle, it comes alive in his hand.

     Answer: *The Castle in the Attic* by Elizabeth Winthrop

10. A ten-year-old girl is kidnapped by a family who have found the fountain of youth.

     Answer: *Tuck Everlasting* by Natalie Babbitt

11. A girl goes into a magic shop where she buys a magic toad.

     Answer: *Jennifer Murdley's Toad* by Bruce Coville.

12. In this fantasy, characters in a place called Coven Tree discover that they must be careful what they wish for.

     Answer: *The Wish Giver* by Bill Brittain

13. A boy climbs aboard a giant fruit and has wonderful adventures with a grasshopper, a centipede, an earthworm, and a spider.

    Answer: *James and the Giant Peach* by Roald Dahl

14. A donkey turns into a rock because he makes an unfortunate wish.

    Answer: *Sylvester and the Magic Pebble* by William Steig

15. A young apprentice is trained by a wizard who sits "high in an oak tree looking at the world."

    Answer: *Tomorrow's Wizard* by Patricia MacLachlan

16. A boy finds a spell in his father's diary that releases magic creatures from an old carpet.

    Answer: *The Genie of Sutton Place* by George Selden

17. Silver shoes, an emerald palace, and flying monkeys all become magic objects and creatures in this classic fantasy.

    Answer: *The Wonderful Wizard of Oz* by L. Frank Baum

18. In the fantasy kingdom in this book, it is "always winter but never Christmas."

    Answer: *The Lion, the Witch, and the Wardrobe* by C. S. Lewis

8

What's Your Story: Biographies of Children's Writers and Illustrators

Biographies can be the perfect link to hook potential readers because they contain stories (the heart of fiction) with factual information (the core of nonfiction). Because many boys in the middle elementary grades turn to nonfiction books, biographies will give them nitty-gritty facts about someone's life. Girls and some boys continue to enjoy fiction because they love narratives with interesting characters and a compelling plot. Biographies written today succeed when they do just that.

With an overwhelming number of biographies and biography series published today, I decided to focus on one subset of this genre: biographies of children's book creators. Children seem to be continually interested in the lives of their favorite book authors and illustrators. Fortunately, there are many exciting resources to satisfy their questions and keep kids reading biographies and also reach for books written by these talented writers and artists.

Many picture books and longer fiction are thinly veiled partial biographies or autobiographies. Cynthia Rylant's homespun story *When I Was Young in the Mountains* describes her Appalachian childhood with a nostalgic tone. Patricia Polacco's numerous picture books reveal fascinating parts of the author/illustrator's early life in such books as *The Bee Tree*; *Thank You, Mr. Falker;* and *My Rotten Red Headed Older Brother.* Laura Ingalls Wilder's perennially popular "Little House" books are fictionalized accounts of the author's own life. Because authors often draw episodes from their own lives when they write fiction, the list could become endless for this chapter. Instead, the titles listed in this bibliography focuses on books written and promoted as biographies or autobiographies.

Many educational publishers offer extensive lists of author biographies in book and video formats. I have included a small number of these and decided to focus on the most distinctive titles rather than list books I feel tend to be formulaic. One exception is the list offered by Richard C. Owen Publishers. These short author and illustrator autobiographies combine full-color photographs and illustrations with lively writing, and the titles are winners.

In the past, children were less interested in school assignments about getting to know authors when teachers expected them to write the author. Jack, a boy in Sharon Creech's *Love That Dog,* is less than excited about writing the author Walt Dean Myers at first. Leigh Botts halfheartedly writes letters to Mr. Henshaw in Beverly Cleary's Newbery Award–winning book. I have heard numerous children over the years complain about these school assignments. But with the advent of the Internet, learning about writers and e-mailing favorite creators is not the dreaded task it once was. I have compiled a selected list of author Web sites for this chapter, and many of them list e-mail addresses so children can make their own direct contacts.

Today reading books about authors is "hot stuff," in the words of young readers. Some of this interest, I think, is the result of school districts, library systems, and bookstores promoting author visits. Not all children, of course, live in metropolitan areas where a steady stream of popular authors and illustrators visit each year. Other kids in St. Paul, Minnesota, or Kansas City, Missouri, for example, can meet and visit with authors at the Red Balloon Children's Bookshop or the Reading Reptile. Kids in smaller cities and rural areas do plan author/writer's conferences at which aspiring young authors meet a guest writer and gain inspiration for their dreams.

Reading biographies of writers and illustrators provides wonderful models for children who think they could create a book. The majority of these celebrities extol the virtues of reading books to help kids become future authors. Illustrators often tell children they drew pictures from their earliest memories. Other creators, just like some kids, were "late bloomers." Chris Crutcher, for example, admits that he only read one book, *To Kill a Mockingbird*, in high school. Dav Pilkey watched TV and drew most of the time. Newbery Award–winning author Jerry Spinelli talks more about his interest in Western movies and sports in his autobiography. Teachers and librarians can find a wide range of author stories to catch the interest of their students.

The information and program ideas in this chapter will help children's librarians in schools and public facilities plan reading programs and activities on the topic of biography from different viewpoints. The "Author Visits" school program can be an actual visit from an author or a virtual visit with children using the Internet and staging their own author interviews in the classroom. The Author Birthday Party program in public libraries offers various ways to celebrate the lives and works of popular children's authors and illustrators. School and public libraries may share resources to do these programs cooperatively during times of tight budgets. The end result is promoting reading and artistic creation for kids today who could be writers and artists in tomorrow's world.

Bibliography

Note: In contrast to simply listing Web site information about authors and illustrators, I have provided longer annotations to the autobiographies in print form in this chapter.

Cleary, Beverly. *My Own Two Feet.* Morrow Junior, 1995.
Describes the author's college years, marriage to Clarence, and her early years as a children's librarian. This volume ends as Beverly begins writing children's books in the 1940s. Her story continues in the sequel *A Girl from Yamhill* (Morrow, 1988).

Byars, Betsy. *The Moon and I.* Julian Messner, 1991.
Betsy admits to always having loved pets of all kinds—including snakes, which made her different from most young girls. The book's title refers to "Moon," her pet snake. A great reader, Betsy says she gets many book ideas from her own reading. Her formula includes devising a plot with possibilities, writing characters to make the plot happen, making the setting believable, and including lots of "scraps."

Fritz, Jean. *Surprising Myself.* Richard C. Owen, 1992.
This short and illuminating autobiography tells about the author's early years in China beside the Yangtse River and her present life in Dobbs Ferry, New York, beside the Hudson. She loves rivers, digging into history and feels that people from the past speak to her. From this background, Fritz has become a noted author of lively biographies for children. Children will be fascinated to know that the author puts her manuscripts in the refrigerator when she is away from home because

she thinks this is a safe place. A longer autobiography about the author's early life in China is the fictionalized account titled *Homesick: My Own Story* (Putnam, 1982).

Goble, Paul. *Hau Kola-Hello Friend*. Richard C. Owen, 1994.

Although this author/illustrator of books about Native Americans was born in England, he now makes his home in Lincoln, Nebraska. Unlike many contemporary authors, Goble admits he does not use much technology, preferring to write on a typewriter. A careful researcher, he takes great care to talk to many native people along with his library work so that he does not make "rude mistakes" about his subject matter.

Howe, James. *Playing with Words*. Richard C. Owen, 1994.

Challenged by a very verbal family, Howe admits the only way he could keep up with his three older brothers was to make them laugh. This sense of humor paid off when he began to write books at age thirty. Watching vampire movies on television contributed to his creating Bunnicula, the vampire rabbit in his book of the same title. Howe, his wife, and their daughter all do writing and photography in their own offices in the family home.

Kuskin, Karla. *Thoughts, Pictures, and Words*. Richard C. Owen, 1995.

Living in New York and Virginia keeps this author commuting to write and stay close to her husband who has an apartment in Arlington, Virginia. She is an illustrator as well as poet and prose writer who admits to keeping a messy workroom because it is filled with all her favorite things. The workroom reminds her of her "attic like" mind that is filled with thoughts and images.

Lowry, Lois. *Looking Back*. Houghton Mifflin, 1998.

Brief vignettes and numerous photographs tell details of the author's life. Quirky stories include the one about Lois putting a wayward mouse in a warm oven when she was a child only for her mother to notice something strange baking. Lois describes a special book game she played with her children in which they would look for sights and people that reminded them of books as they took family walks. Reading and being read to are two of the most important things to her.

Mahy, Margaret. *My Mysterious World*. Richard C. Owen, 1995.

Living in New Zealand, this popular author keeps many unusual animals. An early riser, she begins work at her computer before dawn, takes breaks for meals and returns to write for the remainder of the day. She loves living by the sea, gardening, and answering letters from young readers.

McKissack, Patricia. *Can You Imagine?* Richard C. Owen, 1997.

Born in Tennessee, Patricia's family moved to St. Louis, Missouri, when she was a child. Because her parents divorced and moved apart when she was young, Patricia spent her young life between Nashville and St. Louis. Both families influenced her writing because they were great storytellers. She writes many books her husband Fred researches and describes her writing as "noodling," which is something like "doodling in your head."

Polacco, Patricia. *Firetalking*. Richard C. Owen, 1994.

Patricia's life began in Michigan, although she was raised in California. In this fascinating autobiography, the talented author/illustrator admits her books come mostly from her own life and were influenced by her family of storytellers. Visual art was her first field of study, and although she later earned a doctorate in art history, as a child she had difficulty learning because of dyslexia.

Spinelli, Jerry. *Knots in My Yo Yo String*. Knopf, 1998.

The Newbery Award–winning novelist describes his boyhood in Norristown, Pennsylvania. He describes his "real kid" activities from playing in alleyways and catching salamanders to baseball and going to cowboy movies.

Uchida, Yoshiko. *The Invisible Thread*. Julian Messner, 1991.

This Japanese American author writes stories from her own heritage. She had an especially difficult childhood because her family was held in a Nevada concentration camp during World War II. Yoshi, her nickname, says that she and her siblings felt an "invisible thread" with their Japanese heritage that taught positive values of loyalty, honor, self-discipline, and respect for elders. She was well educated at the University of California, Berkley, and at Smith College and later studied in Japan on a Ford Foundation fellowship. She admits that as an adult she still suffers from the early trauma of growing up in the prison camp.

Yep, Laurence. *The Lost Garden*. Julian Messner, 1991.

In this detailed memoir, Yep returns to the apartment building where he grew up in San Francisco. Now a parking garage, the place of his childhood was actually rundown even though the family called it "the garden." The author's background consists of two cultures from the East and West as he lived in Chinatown for some of his growing up years with his grandmother. Laurence experienced prejudice from the Western culture of his boyhood as well as from his own family because he was not athletic as they were. A student interested in both science and literature, he is a prolific author who draws from both of these backgrounds. He and his wife Joanne Ryder are both writers who have developed their own distinctive voices.

Learning about Authors and Illustrators from the Web

Kids' funny questions, authors' chatty comments with scrapbook photo formats, and full-color posters based on illustrators' books represent the variety of exciting Web sites kids will love to explore on this topic. The Web pages generally have less in-depth information than author biographies, but they can be clever and very creative. Illustrator/authors such as Dav Pilkey, Jan Brett, and Patricia Polacco share their personal stories and treat children to an abundance of activity pages.

The tone of most author sites is so informal and personal that students will feel as if the celebrity is speaking directly to them. This conversational style, especially if an e-mail address is included, creates the impression that children in any part of the country are actually having a visit with the author. Certainly this electronic experience cannot replace the excitement of hosting a popular author or illustrator in your community, but it is cheaper and more readily available. No longer will children think of book creators as distant figures whose lives are far removed from the real world. The sprightly author Jon Scieszka reminds us that today's writers may be much more like "real people" than revered authors from the past.

Some Web sites are created and maintained by publishers or educational groups. Although they tend to have less information and are formal in presentational style, they cover authors and illustrators who are not listed separately in author directories of Web sites. Some of these include the following:

www.eduplace.com/author

www.harperchildrens.com

www.penguinputnam.com

www.randomhouse.com

http://teacher.scholastic.com/writewit/biography/biography

www.scottforesman.com

I have tried to include a wide variety of authors and illustrators from different ethnic backgrounds but was disappointed not to find as much diversity as I had hoped. The publisher sites just listed did provide information about some authors who do not keep their own sites. Thus, I learned that Sharon Bell

Mathias frequently visited the library as a child and read on the fire escape outside the kitchen in her family's apartment home. Patricia and Frederick McKissack's pages under the Scholastic site not only describe this writing team's work habits but also provide guidance to students in writing biographies about other people.

The majority of the Web pages that follow are individual author or illustrator sites. These, of course, change constantly, so any attempt to be comprehensive is impossible. At the time of writing this chapter, I have searched these sites personally.

Judy Blume: www.judyblume.com

Jan Brett: www.janbrett.com

Marc Brown: www.twbookmark.com

Eric Carle: www.eric-carle.com/

Nancy Carlson: www.nancycarlson.com

Beverly Cleary: www.beverlycleary.com

Sharon Creech: www.sharoncreech.com

Tomie dePaola: www.tomie.com

Gail Gibbons: www.gailgibbons.com/

Jamie Gilson: www.jamiegilson.com

Gail Haley: www.gailhaley.com/

Will Hobbs: www.willhobbsauthor.com/

Diana Wynne Jones: www.dianawynnejones.com

Loreen Leedy: www.loreenleedy.com

Ursula LeGuin: www.ursulaleguin.com

Julius Lester: www.eduplace.com/kids/hmr/mtai/lester.html

Lois Lowry: www.loislowry.com

Laura Numeroff: www.lauranumberoff.com/

Margie Palatini: www.margiepalatini.com

Katherine Paterson: www.terabithia.com

Gary Paulsen: www.randomhouse.com

Dav Pilkey: www.pilkey.com

Patricia Polacco: www.patriciapolacco.com/

Faith Ringgold: www.faithringgold.com

J. K. Rowling: www.jkrowling.com/

Pam Munoz Ryan: www.pammunozryan.com

Gary Soto: www.garysoto.com

The following Web sites provide directories to other children's book authors and illustrators, links to related sites, and some critical data:

Bethany Roberts Directory of Children's Book Authors and Illustrators on the Web from A to Z: www.bethanyroberts.com/childrensbookauthorsA-Z.htm

Children's Book Council, About Authors and Illustrators: www.cbcbooks.org/html/aboutauthors. html

Children's Literature Web Guide: www.childrensliterature.com

Kay E. Vandergrift. Learning about the Author and Illustrator Pages: www.sclis.rutgers.edu/ kvander/authorsite

Author Visits: A Program for Schools

Whether an author actually comes to your school or the author visit is a media visit by e-mail or phone, the various activities described here will prepare children for knowing something about authors and illustrators of children's books. If you are planning an actual author visit, consult the "Planning an Author Visit" document in the appendix of this book.

Materials Needed

1. Class scrapbook and extra pages

Procedure

1. Ask children to research one author or several authors by selecting books from the bibliography of this chapter and researching the Internet. If the entire class researches the same author, materials will need to be shared. The teacher may assign specific parts of an author's life to each child or a group of children. Assign different books by the author to various children.

2. Assuming that several authors will be researched, assign a different author or illustrator to each child.

   Give children copies of the "A Visit with the Author/Illustrator" scrapbook page from this chapter. Kids complete this page and add extra materials of their own using individual creativity. Compile all student pages into a class scrapbook that can be kept in the school library media center.

3. As students are conducting their research, have them read at least one book written or illustrated by this author or illustrator.

4. Give children one of two options. Option I: Assume the role of the author and have another student interview you in front of the class. (Sample interview questions appear later in the chapter to guide students.) Option II: Pretend you are the guest author you have researched. Give a short speech (about five to eight minutes) to the class as if you are this celebrated guest. Tell about your life and something about the books you have written and provide advice for would-be authors.

5. Prepare an "Author's Advice" Board for each student to submit a quote or comment from various authors. A sample advice page appears in this chapter.

Sample Interview Questions
for an Author/Illustrator

1. Where were you born, and where did you grow up?

2. In what ways did these places influence your writing (or your art)?

3. Did you like school?

4. What were your favorite subjects?

5. Did you like to read? What were your favorite books when you were growing up?

6. What were your favorite activities or interests then?

7. Did you have other jobs or careers before you became an author or artist?

8. When and why did you decide to become a writer (or an illustrator)?

9. Did you receive special training to write (or illustrate)?

10. What is your favorite book (or books) that you have created? Why?

11. Where do you write?

12. What do you like best about creating books? What do you like least?

13. Where do you get your ideas?

14. Do you have any advice for people who want to write or illustrate books?

A Visit with the Author

Author's Birthplace and Home:

Picture of Author

Author's Favorite Things or People from Childhood:

Author's Favorite Things to Do Today:

Author's Books (Pictures of Covers)

Author's Advice for Young Writers:

Ideas—Thoughts—Brainstorms—Inspiration—Secrets—Ideas and More!

Happy Birthday Dear Author: A Program for Public Libraries

Although this program can be focused around a single author with book readings and activities related to that author, this program has been planned as a general party for many children's book authors and illustrators. Using the Web sites and ideas in this chapter, the librarian may wish to include whatever authors she wishes.

Materials Needed

1. Party invitations, if desired

2. Balloons

3. Crepe paper streamers

4. Several poster boards for making large wall calendars

5. Art paper for making the birthday hat game

6. Construction paper, multiple scissors, glue, markers, boxes of author pictures for making scrapbooks

7. Index cards, large box, wrapping paper and ribbons for the birthday surprise box

8. Colored paper and markers for making birthday cards

9. Juice and purchased sheet cake

Procedure

1. Prepare for the Authors' Birthday Party by sending out invitations or using an invitation format for publicity.

2. Decorate the program room for a birthday party with plenty of balloons and streamers. For fun, write the name of an author or illustrator on each balloon and give these away to children as they leave the event.

3. Make a huge calendar display with space to write in the names of authors on various days. As an alternative, make a chart of each month of the year and list the names of authors and illustrators born during the appropriate months.

4. Encourage children to come dressed as their favorite author or illustrator or as a character from a favorite children's book. For example, a girl could dress in bright colors, wear her hair piled on top of her head, and carry an artist's palette to resemble Patricia Polacco. A boy dressed as a magician could be playing the part of Sid Fleischman. Character costumes might include a foam-cheese-headed child for the Stinky Cheese Man, or a mouse-eared girl with red boots and carrying a purple purse for Lily from Kevin Henkes's book *Lily's Purple Plastic Purse*.

5. Play alternative versions of standard birthday party games such as Pin the Birthday Hat on the Author. Any hat shape cut from paper with a birthday candle taped on it will serve as the birthday hat. Cut out a large oval shape for the author's head and add photograph collage pictures of various authors that are printed from Internet photographs.

6. Read beginnings of several novels and picture books by popular authors. Ask children to guess who wrote the book and identify the title. This does not need to be a game with rewards. Explain to children that everyone will receive a birthday party favor at the end of the party.

7. Because kids love to make scrapbooks, provide each program participant with construction paper, scissors, markers, and glue. Fill several boxes full of author photos, flyers, book advertisements, and other publicity pieces that the librarian can order from different book publishers. Photos and activity pages from authors can be printed from Web sites given in this chapter. Print plenty of these to have available for children's scrapbooks for this activity.

8. Play the game "Open the Birthday Surprise Box" by writing questions about popular authors, illustrators, and books on different colors of index cards with the answer written on the back. Place cards in a big box that is wrapped up to look like a birthday present. Add a showy bow for fun. Sample questions appear in this chapter under the section "Birthday Surprise Box Questions."

9. Sing "Happy Birthday Dear Author" to the traditional birthday song tune.

10. If time permits, let children make birthday cards for authors whose birthdays happen during the month of your program. A list of birthdays for many popular authors appears in this chapter.

11. Enjoy juice and a sheet cake ordered from a local bakery or grocery store. Distribute party favors such as fancy bookmarks, coupons for a discount from local bookstores, or individual birthday cupcakes to take home.

Birthday Surprise Box Questions (Stated as answers, similar to the television game show *Jeopardy*)

1. He grew up in New York, but his Newbery Award–winning book is set in a "character building" camp in the West.

    Answer: Louis Sachar
    Bonus: What is the name of this book?
    Answer: *Holes*

2. She has won the Newbery Medal three times. She had "beginner's luck" because the first book she wrote was a Newbery Honor Book and the second book she wrote won the Newbery Medal in the same year!

    Answer: Elaine Koningsburg
    Bonus: What were the names of these two books?
    Answer: Honor: *Jennifer, Hecate, Macbeth, William McKinley and Me, Elizabeth*
    Medal: *From the Mixed Up Files of Mrs. Basil E. Frankweiller*

3. Born in Ireland, she writes fiction and nonfiction books. Many of her picture books concern social issues, such as one set during the riots in Los Angeles.

    Answer: Eve Bunting

4. Author of stories for children and young adults, one of her most popular characters is named for a kind of chocolate candy.

    Answer: Judy Blume
    Bonus: What was the name of this character?
    Answer: Fudge

5. An illustrator and author of many books about a shy aardvark and his bossy sister.

    Answer: Marc Brown

6. This Japanese American illustrator/author won a Caldecott Medal for a book about his grandfather's journey to America.

    Answer: Allen Say

7. This African American author wrote a book about a boy who searches for his father's identity. He thinks his dad was a jazz musician. The book won the Newbery Medal and the Coretta Scott King Award in the same year.

    Answer: Christopher Paul Curtis
    Bonus: What was the name of this book?
    Answer: *Bud, Not Buddy*

8. This writer was a sports nut when he was a kid, and his Newbery Medal Book told exaggerated stories about a kid who loved baseball and candy.

    Answer: Jerry Spinelli
    Bonus: What was the name of this book?
    Answer: *Maniac McGee*

9. This author's most famous book is an animal fantasy with a pig and a spider as main characters.

    Answer: E. B. White
    Bonus: What was the name of this book?
    Answer: *Charlotte's Web*

10. She writes easy-to-read books about a boy and his pet dog.

    Answer: Cynthia Rylant
    Bonus: What is the name of this boy and his dog?
    Answer: Henry and Mudge

11. This author got into so much trouble in school that his teacher moved his desk to the hall where he could draw cartoons as much as he liked.

    Answer: Dav Pilkey

12. This Japanese American author grew up in a prison camp in Nevada and wrote her autobiography titled *The Invisible Thread.*

    Answer: Yoshiko Uchi

13. This Newbery Award–winning author writes humorous stories and also some very thoughtful ones. One of her award-winning books concerns a Jewish girl who lives secretly with a gentile family in Denmark during World War II.

    Answer: Lois Lowry
    Bonus: What is the name of this book?
    Answer: *Number the Stars*

14. She is a naturalist who has written several books about an Alaskan animal she grew to love.

> Answer: Jean Craighead George

15. He uses only one name as an author, is a twin, and wrote a Newbery Medal book about a boy during the Middle Ages.

> Answer: Avi
> Bonus: What is the name of this book?
> Answer: *Crispin: The Cross of Lead*

16. She writes funny books and poetry. One of her most popular books is based on her younger son Alexander, who had lots of bad days.

> Answer: Judith Viorst
> Bonus: What was the name of the book?
> Answer: *Alexander and the Terrible, Horrible, No Good Very Bad Day*

17. His real name is Daniel Handler. His darkly humorous books are about the misfortunes of the Baudelaire children.

> Answer: Lemony Snicket

18. This Chinese American Author lives in San Francisco with his wife, who is also a writer.

> Answer: Laurence Yep

19. Her autobiography *The Moon and I* is about her life and her pet snake, not about the heavenly body.

> Answer: Betsy Byars

20. He loves magic tricks and was a magician before he became an author of children's books.

> Answer: Sid Fleischman

21. Two of his popular fantasy books are set inside a chocolate factory and inside a peach.

> Answer: Roald Dahl

Birthdays of Selected Authors and Illustrators

You will find a longer list of author and illustrator birthdays on Kathy Schrock's Guide for Educators. Here is her Web site: School.discovery.com/schrockguide/authordate.html

January

18—A. A. Milne
29—Bill Peet
30—Lloyd Alexander
31—Gerald McDermott

February

1—Jerry Spinelli
2—Judith Viorst
7—Laura Ingalls Wilder
10—Elaine Koningsburg
11—Jane Yolen
12—Judy Blume

March

2—Dr. Seuss
4—Dav Pilkey
12—Virginia Hamilton
16—Sid Fleischman
20—Lois Lowry, Louis Sachar

April

2—Hans Christian Andersen
5—Richard Peck
12—Beverly Cleary

May

9—Sir James Barrie
15—L. Frank Baum
16—Bruce Coville
23—Susan Cooper

June

6—Cynthia Rylant
10—Maurice Sendak
14—Laurence Yep
18—Chris Van Allsburg, Angela Johnson
25—Eric Carle
27—Louise Clifton

July

2—Jean Craighead George
11—E. B. White, Patricia Polacco
13—Ashley Bryan
14—Peggy Parish, Laura Numeroff
19—Eve Merriam
28—Natalie Babbitt
29—Sharon Creech
31—J. K. Rowling

August

1—Gail Gibbons
7—Betsy Byars
9—Patricia McKissack
16—Matt Christopher
28—Allen Say

September

8—Jon Scieszka
13—Roald Dahl, Mildred D. Taylor
15—Tomie dePaola
17—Paul Goble

October

4—Karen Cushman, Susan Meddaugh
8—Faith Ringgold
10—Nancy Carlson
20—Ursula K. Le Guin
25—Steven Kellogg
30—Katherine Paterson

November

9—Lois Ehlert, Pat Cummings
16—Jean Fritz
24—Yoshiko Uchida
25—Marc Brown
27—Kevin Henkes
28—Ed Young
29—Madeleine L'Engle, C. S. Lewis

December

1—Jan Brett
9—Mary Downing Hahn
19—Eve Bunting

Author Advice Board

Use these authors' quotes on a display board or the bulletin board for the school program or for a display in the public library.

- "Read, read, read, read, read. . . . You learn how to write by reading—reading just everything. My second bit of advice is that you have to know grammar. . . . The art of writing is how to write a good sentence. My final words of advice are rewrite, rewrite, rewrite, rewrite. . . . The way you write it the first time is seldom the best that it can be." (Julius Lester)

- "When I talk to children and aspiring writers, I always ask them to listen to the voice [inside of them], turn off the television and listen . . . listen . . . listen." (Patricia Polacco)

- "I read everything. My favorite things to read are fairy tales, myths, and legends." (Jon Scieszka)

- "Like anything else in life, if you're serious about it [writing], do it everyday. Stay in practice. At first it seems hard, but your mind is so fantastic, it learns how to make it easier." (Christopher Paul Curtis)

- "Think of an idea or topic that is so strong within you that it's going to come out passionately as you write about it. Because that's what shines in a book. And then do a lot of work—reading and research—to add layers to your idea." (Karen Cushman)

- "If you want to illustrate stories—just start right away. And keep drawing . . . you have to practice, practice, practice." (Susan Meddaugh)

9

In the Know: Manners for Kids

After a long absence, books on manners for children have reappeared on library and bookstore shelves. Youth librarians in the 1980s searched for titles to replace older manners books that seemed embarrassingly outmoded. Children needed books to learn basic table manners, how to introduce their friends to adults, and tips on writing good thank you letters. Kids often forget to say the magic words "please," "thank you," and "I'm sorry" if they are not reminded to do so in stories and in guidebooks. Yet librarians, teachers, and concerned parents were hard pressed to find relevant titles during those years of radical social change in our country. Wearing white gloves and always opening doors for women were considered artificial throw backs to Victorian days for many young people.

The topic of etiquette and manners seems to be so uncomfortable even to address that almost a generation managed to avoid learning basic rules that could help them manage social situations with grace. As a result, many corporations feel compelled to offer workshops in etiquette that, in the past, young people had learned in the home or in the community. Today classes in etiquette for children are offered by community centers, museums, libraries, and even in camps. Schools of protocol and etiquette consultants proliferate. It seems as if we are desperate to catch up, to expose children to this neglected topic that underlies our ability as people to get along with one another. If schools do not include this subject directly in the school curriculum, I would suggest that it relates to the social studies curriculum right along with learning about good citizenship, decision making, and conflict resolution. The ideas found in this chapter will help schools and public libraries plan informative and entertaining programs on the subject.

I have included the subtopic of bullies and bullying in the scope of this chapter because it involves the same basic premise. Treating others as one would want to be treated really is the foundation for understanding manners and for dealing with bullying behavior. Statistics show alarming trends of bullying growing to almost epidemic proportions—not just on playgrounds but in every social setting. Some contend that bullying has always been a problem, but we have become more socially conscious of the consequences. No longer does the "kids will be kids" slogan stand as an acceptable excuse for allowing kids to treat others abusively. Kids who bully and kids who are victims can become adults who bully in boardrooms and angry adults who exhibit passive-aggressive behaviors because they may think of themselves as adult victims. People who casually tell children to "ignore this and it will stop" are not providing kids with useful ways to handle real conflict. Many adults are at a loss themselves in knowing what to do. Fortunately, good books and programs on antibullying exist. Some of these books are included in the bibliography of this chapter.

Research on the topic of manners has produced numerous unhelpful Web sites if one is looking for general information. Flashy videos and ads of etiquette consultants flood the Internet. Too many books of marginal quality fill bookstores and are on sale over the Internet. One has to be careful to select solid titles that do not preach when they teach manners to kids. Overly "cute" illustrations and condescending texts seem to proliferate instead of more down-to-earth books that treat children with respect. This is ironic because books on manners need be the very model of respectful treatment. Generally series books on behavior are not included because most of them tend to be of lesser literary value with sloppy art. The titles included in this chapter's bibliography are among the better choices. Particularly pleasing are such books as *Rules of the Wild* and *This Little Piggy's Book of Manners* that use humor to teach this topic. Children can laugh as they learn and will remember good manners in a more positive way if books are not so heavy handed in their approach.

Teachers and librarians will not find long lists or explanations for manners in particular settings in this chapter. That information is found in books listed in the bibliography. Rather, program activities provide guidelines and springboards for letting children explore the topic.

The program activities in this chapter give children opportunities to engage in role-play and in writing their own guidelines for good behavior. Teacher/librarians will find tips for showing children how to write thank you notes. A placemat showing a proper table setting is included. The Oops Game and antibullying doorknob decorations will give children enjoyable ways to learn behavior models. The script "Mind Your Manners with Miss P.Q." can be the main entertainment for a public library program. The librarian might use this for a single tea party or special event then decide that children like special events every year. In this case, the "Mind Your Manners" script lends itself to repeat performances. Develop your own script, adding new letters and other characters for the fun to continue year after year.

Bibliography

Allen, Kathryn Madeline. *This Little Piggy's Book of Manners.* Illustrated by Nancy Wolff. Henry Holt, 2003.

Some pigs use good manners and others do not in this book with bright gouache illustrations and fun sidebar conversations between the animals. Children could continue the story by writing their own examples of good and bad manners.

Buehner, Caralyn. *I Did It, I'm Sorry.* Illustrated by Mark Buehner. Dial, 1998.

A series of animals from bats to rats are confronted with situations in which they are faced with making moral decisions involving honesty, responsible behaviors, and manners. Young readers are presented with the choices. Answers are given at the back of the book.

Cole, Babette. *The Bad Good Manners Book.* Dial, 1996.

This rhymed text presents a light-hearted look at good manners for kids.

Giblin, James Cross. *From Hand to Mouth or, How We Invented Knives, Forks, Spoons, and Chopsticks & the Table Manners to Go with Them.* Crowell, 1987.

This history of table implements and manners begins almost five thousand years ago and culminates with the rapid changes from the eighteenth century to the twentieth century. Children will be fascinated by why chopsticks were developed, the differences between Continental and American eating styles as well as the laws that forbade sharp knives in a French table setting.

Hazen, Barbara Shook. *Hello Gnu, How Do You Do?* Illustrated by Dara Goldman, Doubleday, 1990.

This introduction to the topic of being polite is divided into such areas as writing thank you notes, manners in public, table manners, and telephone manners.

Holyoke, Nancy. *Oops! The Manners Guide for Girls*. Illustrated by Debbie Tilley. Pleasant Company, 1997.

Profusely illustrated with lots of sidebars, letters, and a breezy style, this guide covers topics from manners at friends' homes, at the table, in public places, when giving gifts, and using the telephone.

Howe, James. *The Muppet Guide to Magnificent Manners*. Illustrated by Peter Elwell. Random House, 1984.

Jim Henson's Muppets teach children manners for parties, using the telephone, writing letters, and other everyday situations in eight short chapters. Examples of both good and bad manners are provided through scripts, letters, and illustrations.

James, Elizabeth, and Carol Barkin. *Social Smarts: Manners for Today's Kids*. Illustrated by Martha Weston. Clarion, 1996.

This up-to-date guide intended for children to read on their own bases various situations—manners at the table, in difficult situations, on the phone, meeting people, and so on—on the concept of the Golden Rule—treating others as you would like to be treated. Including letters from real kids and using a friendly tone, the authors handle tricky situations with ease.

Joslin, Sesyle. *What Do You Say, Dear?* Illustrated by Maurice Sendak. Addison Wesley, 1958.

Playful illustrations and gentle text present the young reader with a series of situations that call for gracious words to be spoken. A knight cuts off a dragon's head for a terrified lass and a bad cowboy asks a boy if he would like a hole shot through his head. The repeated question, "What do you say, dear?" prompts children to answer "thank you" or "no, thank you" as they practice good manners.

Leaf, Munro. *Four-and-Twenty Watchbirds*. Linnet Books, 1990.

Previously published in four little books, these twenty-four watchbirds introduce children with various kinds of bad manners. Examples include the "butter-in," "won't share," "know-it-all," "bragger," "tattle tale," "grabber," "bully," "pouter," and "sneaky." Children will be inspired to make their own catalogue of characters and illustrate them in a style as simple as those by Leaf.

Levin, Bridget. *Rules of the Wild: An Unruly Book of Manners*. Illustrated by Amanda Shepherd. Chronicle, 2004.

Shepherd's whimsically wild drawings perfectly match the rhymed text describing unruly manners through the perspectives of different animals. A piggy, for example, might not be offended by eating piggy portions, nor would bats become disturbed about young bats staying up all night. A snake wouldn't worry about clothes left on the floor nor would a camel mother fuss about spitting. The implication, of course, is that such behavior is upsetting when children try it. This humorous turnabout will inspire children to create their own books of unruly manners naturally!

Marciano, John Bemelmans. *Madeline Says Merci: The-Always-Be-Polite Book*. Viking, 2001.

Different polite words or phrases are followed by short rhyming verses and Madeline illustrations by the grandson of the famous Ludwig Bemelmans.

Mitchell, Mary. *Dear Ms. Demeanor. . . The Young Person's Etiquette Guide to Handling Any Social Situation with Confidence and Grace*. Contemporary Books, 1994.

A former professional etiquette instructor bases her ideas on the larger context of respecting other people. Each chapter addresses a different area—manners at home, with peers, at school, table manners, correspondence. The question-and-answer format establishes a relaxed style between author and reader.

Books on Bullies

Clements, Andrew. *Jake Drake, Bully Buster*. Simon & Schuster, 2001.
    Jake Drake, fourth grader, relates the story of how he became a bully buster in the second grade when Link, a new boy, comes to school and bullies Jake for several months. When Jake learns to work with Link on a social studies project, Jake not only understands Link's behavior, he turns the knowledge into a winning combination for both of them.

Estes, Eleanor. *The Hundred Dresses*. Harcourt Brace, 1972 (originally published in 1944).
    Wanda, recently immigrated from Poland, is teased unmercifully by her classmates for her odd clothes, her name, and her comment that she has one hundred dresses at home in her closet. Eventually, two American children do understand what Wanda means and how they mistreated her. This classic still helps children understand the importance of accepting others who are different from themselves.

Livingston, Irene. *Finklehopper Frog Cheers*. Illustrated by Brian Lies. Tricycle Press, 2005.
    Finklehopper Frog and his friend Ruby Rabbit are afraid of being bullied at the town picnic, but they soon learn by sticking together that they will change the bullies' behavior. The rhyme and slick answers may sound too easy for some older kids, but the examples of good sportsmanship will be helpful to many others.

Ludwig, Trudy. *My Secret Bully*. Illustrated by Abigail Marble. Tricycle Press, 2004.
    This sensitive story targeted at five- to eleven-year-old readers tells about emotional bullying between two girls rather than the physical aggression that is easier to identify. Katie uses name-calling, humiliation, and manipulative behavior to control Monica. When Monica can turn to her mother for guidance, she is able to stop this vicious game.

Middleton-Moz, Jane, and Mary Lee Zawadski. *Bullies from the Playground to the Boardroom*. Health Communications, 2002.
    This practical sourcebook traces bullying behavior from childhood through adulthood. Useful for the educator or parent, it suggests strategies for coping with and reaching bullies as well as providing insights for victims to face past abuses to which they have been subjected.

Myers, Christopher. *Wings*. Scholastic, 2000.
    Ikarus Johnson, a black child in a large city, wears wings to school. Classmates taunt and bully him, but Ikarus uses his wings to gain his own sense of identity.

O'Neill, Alexis. *The Recess Queen*. Illustrated by Laura Huliska-Beith. Scholastic, 2002.
    All the kids in school are terrified of Mean Jean, the class bully, until the intrepid Katie Sue challenges Mean Jean on the playground. This lively picture book will appeal to elementary school–age children from younger to older and can be read interactively with groups.

Romain, Trevor. *Bullies Are a Pain in the Brain*. Free Spirit, 1997.
    Despite the poorly executed cartoon cover art, this guide has lots of practical strategies for dealing with bullies. It explodes many myths and helps in understanding truths about bullies. The interior cartoon art will have child appeal.

Wells, Rosemary. *Hazel's Amazing Mother*. Dial Books, 1985.
    Hazel's beloved doll Eleanor is snatched away and ruined by three bullies only to be mended and restored when Hazel's amazing mother arrives on the scene. This lesson in comeuppance is humorously told with whimsy and panache.

In the Know: A School Program about Manners

Classroom teachers can use this program in units about communities, social studies, or bullies. School librarians along with classroom teachers can use it. The games and writing activities encourage role-playing games and writing.

Materials Needed

1. Paper for thank you notes

2. Photocopies of table settings

3. Heavy paper and photocopies of bully doorknob decorations

4. Multiple pairs of scissors, markers

Procedure

1. Introduce the topic by reading one of the books from the bibliography about manners. Younger students will relate to *Rules of the Wild* or *Madeline Says Merci.* Older students might need a more "breezy" approach with the teacher/librarian reading from some of the letters in *Social Smarts.*

2. Give students opportunities to play the game of "Oops!" and do role-playing with situations described in "Playing Fair, Showing Care."

3. Use the letters in the "Thank You Notes" exercise to give students the opportunity to write thank you letters and notes.

4. Post the "In the Know: Things to Think About and Act Upon" messages around the library or classroom. Encourage students to write their own "In the Know" thoughts.

5. Photocopy the sample place-setting page (Figure 9.1) so that children can practice proper table settings. Children make want to make their own tablemats with this design to take home.

6. Photocopy the two bullies doorknob decorations (Figures 9.2 and 9.3) on card stock or heavier-weight paper. Encourage kids to color these and cut them out. Class members can hang them on doors around the school, at home, and in community centers to pass along the word that bully behavior is not tolerated by kids "in the know."

The Oops! Game

This game gives children an opportunity to learn more about manners by answering a series of questions. Divide the class into two groups. The teacher/librarian reads aloud a series of situations that may or may not show good manners. If the situation demonstrates good manners, students respond, "Yes!" If poor manners are shown, students respond, "Oops!" Correct responses receive one point. When a student explains how the poor manners can be improved, two additional points are given. Rather than allow the entire team to respond, "Yes" or "Oops" at the same time, each team should appoint a single responder. The team receiving the most points is declared winner. Perhaps teacher can provide a reward for the winning team to share with everyone.

The following situation cards serve as examples of ones teachers or students can create to play this game.

Situation: The Birthday Gift

Amy's aunt gave her a green sweater for her birthday. Amy hates green but she wanted to be honest when she wrote a thank you note. Amy told her aunt that she wished the sweater was purple instead.

Answer: Oops!

Improvement: Amy shouldn't say anything about not liking green but thank her aunt for the sweater.

Situation: Introductions

Adam introduced his friend Ben and his grandma. Adam said, "Ben, this is my grandma. Grandma, this is Ben."

Answer: Oops!

Improvement: Grandma is older than Ben, so Adam needs to introduce Ben to his grandma. He should have said, "Grandma, this is my friend Ben. Ben, this is my grandma, Mrs. Allen." (By giving grandma's name, "Mrs. Allen," Adam is helping Ben to know what to call her other than "Grandma.")

Situation: Napkins on the Table

Martha wiped her hands on the napkin beside her fork then folded the napkin and put it back on the table.

Answer: Oops!

Improvement: Martha should have put her napkin in her lap, then used it to wipe her hands and replaced it in her lap.

Situation: Salad on the Table

Sara sat down at the dinner table at her friend's house. There were salad plates filled with salad already on the table. Sara ate all of her salad then she looked up to see that no one else had touched theirs.

Answer: Oops!

Improvement: Wait for the hostess to begin eating. Maybe another course of food will be served before the salad.

Situation: Magic Words

Matt's dad gave him a ride to the movies to meet his friends. Matt said, "Bye, Dad. See ya later," then slammed the car door.

Answer: Oops!

Improvement: What about using those magic words "thank you"?

Situation: Talking at the Movies

Mike and his buddies were making jokes and talking during a movie when a woman behind them said, "Quiet down there, boys!" Mike got mad and just kept on talking.

Answer: Oops!

Improvement: Mike made a mistake by talking, and he only made it worse by not stopping. Mike should have apologized and been quiet.

Playing Fair, Showing Care: A Role-Playing Exercise

Give students the experience of practicing good behavior and manners with these role-playing exercises. Rather than just teaching children rules of good table manners and etiquette in social situations, these exercises are designed to help young people empathize with the feelings of others. The true foundation for manners lies in the old Golden Rule: treat others the way you wish to be treated. These examples will help students and teachers create their own situations for further practice.

If you have not tried role-playing with students, try giving the kids some beginning lines and coaching them to use their own words in working through the situation as they might do in their own lives. Emphasize that there is no right or wrong way to do this. The idea is to be able to show the feelings of the characters in these exercises. If students are shy about doing this in front of a class, divide the class into small groups with a student or adult volunteer acting as a coach.

Party Time

Situation: Kathy was having a Halloween party for her friends. Karen heard Susan and Amy talking about receiving invitations. Karen thought she was a friend of Kathy's, too. She felt left out but was too embarrassed to ask Kathy about the party. (Choose four people to take the roles and act out this situation.)

New Kid in the Class

Situation: Jason, a fourth grader, moved to Middletown from a small town out of state. He wants to make friends with the other kids in his class, but they seem unfriendly to him. The day after he arrives, he overhears three boys talking about him in whispers. (Choose four people to take the roles and act out this situation. By the end of this exercise, have the kids find a positive way to include Jason in the group.)

Name Calling

Situation: Emma's mother picked her up from school in the family's brand new sports car. Emma's friends became so jealous, they wouldn't speak directly to her the next day. By the third day, one former friend called Emma a "show-off." By the next day several other kids called her "show-off" too. (Choose four or five students to take the roles of Emma and the other classmates. By the end of this reenactment, find a way for the name-calling to stop without having an adult intervene.)

Science Project

Situation: Joe brought his science project to school a week early because his mother said his little brother couldn't be trusted to keep his hands off of the display. Just as Joe got to school, a bully from his class grabbed the project. He ran off down the hall telling Joe that he was going to turn in the project as his own. (Select two or more students to role-play this situation. The situation needs to end with a positive resolution.)

Telephone Talk

Situation: Mrs. Murphy calls the Duncan family. She wishes to speak with Mrs. Duncan, who is not home. Jonas Duncan answers the phone rudely. Mrs. Murphy tries to get Jonas to take a message, but he is uncooperative. Finally Jonas takes the message, but he and Mrs. Murphy end the conversation on an unpleasant note. (Choose two students to reenact this conversation. Then have the students role-play the situation with Jonas acting politely instead of rudely.)

Using a Cell Phone in the Library

Situation: Tim's mother called him on his cell phone after school. Tim was at the library when his phone rang. His mother was upset because he was to come straight home after school. She was almost yelling through the phone. Tim's voice got loud, too. A person in the library complained to the librarian, so Tim was really in trouble. (Choose three or more students to role-play this situation.)

In the Know—Things to Think About and Act Upon

- Littering Makes the World Ugly.
- Bad Language Bothers Others.
- Be Cool, Not Cruel.
- Be Careful with People and Things.
- Accept Praise and Pass It On!
- Offer to Help, Then Do Something!
- Courtesy Begins at Home.
- Graffiti Is Gross.
- Kindness Begins with Me.
- Following the Herd Can Land You in a Bad Place—Caution!

In the Know—On the Phone

- Speak slowly and clearly, especially when leaving messages on voicemail.

- Speak in a well-modulated voice, neither too loud nor too soft.

- Ask to take a message if the person to whom the caller wishes to speak is not there.

- Use cell phones in appropriate places (not in libraries or other quiet places).

- Be polite instead of "cute" or sassy.

Thank You Note Tip Sheet

1. Written thank you notes are always considerate ways to thank people for gifts you receive. E-mail is not as thoughtful.

    (Spoken thanks are nice but not the same!)

2. Always praise the gift, even if you don't like it.

    (Aunt Emily doesn't know you hate orange sweatshirts!)

3. Think of something specific about the gift to comment on.

    ("I like the design on the jacket you sent. It is fun!")

4. Add a little news or comment besides the thank you to make your note more interesting.

    ("I enjoyed my birthday party at the bowling alley. Dad says you enjoy bowling, too.")

5. Thank the giver both at the beginning and end of the note. It makes the giver feel extra appreciated.

Figure 9.1

Figure 9.2

Figure 9.3

You Are Invited: A Holiday Tea Party or Special Party for Public Libraries

Enjoy the winter holidays when children are out of school with a tea party for children older than the preschool set. To make this a festive event, ask parents to preregister their children so you can set the tables with good china or nice paper plates in an attractive setting. Specify that dress-up clothes are appropriate to wear for this occasion. Seating children at tables and asking them to wear their better clothes often sets the mood for something a little more formal where good manners are practiced. The real fun of the event features a short play "Mind Your Manners with Miss P.Q."

Materials Needed

1. China or nice paper plates and cups for table settings

2. Table decorations and napkins

3. Refreshments such as fruit-flavored tea, cookies, and tea sandwiches, enough to feed the number of children you will be accepting. (This number will depend on the size of your program room and the number of staff and volunteers you will have. I suggest limiting the number to thirty or forty children. If the event becomes so popular you are turning away children, you may wish to schedule two parties on the same day.)

Procedure

1. The Miss P.Q. character or the librarian (if the librarian is not playing this part) should greet each child as he or she arrives. Teens may act as hostesses and hosts to seat children at preset tables.

2. Miss P.Q. welcomes everyone to the event and then announces that food will be served. Hostesses/hosts pour tea and bring in trays of cookies and sandwiches. Miss P.Q. goes from table to table as she chats with the party guests and facilitates conversation between children at the table. Kids may need a little guidance in introducing themselves at the tables.

3. After refreshments are served, hostesses remove the dishes.

4. The librarian reads a book or two such as *Rules of the Wild* or *Madeline Says Merci.* Several other people may read poems about manners, good and bad, from a collection of poems by Shel Silverstein or Jack Prelutsky.

5. Miss P.Q. and her friends perform the play "Mind Your Manners."

6. Party guests are thanked as the party ends.

Mind Your Manners with Miss P.Q.

Adapt the following script as you like. The Miss P.Q. character should dress flamboyantly; perhaps she should wear a large hat, white gloves, and a party dress. If the librarian does not feel this flamboyant, a high school student or local actress could play the part. Certainly, a man who would use the name "Mr. P.Q. Manners" could play the part.

Miss P.Q.:   How do you do, children! My name is Miss P.Q. Manners. I'm here to help you mind your P's and Q's. You know—P's and Q's? Why, they are all the things you should remember if you practice good manners. Welcome to our Holiday tea party. We are sooooo glad you came! Thank you for coming and I thank all the people who helped me plan this party. [Here is your opportunity to model good manners for children!]

You know, many children write Miss P.Q. questions about good manners. I always love to get letters, don't you? I've saved some of the best letters children have sent to me. Would you like to hear them?

Good! Let's get started. I've brought along my friends Fancy Nancy and Smart Art to read aloud some of the letters.

Nancy, would you like to begin?

Nancy: Oh yes, Miss P.Q. I would just looooove to read one of your lovely letters.

Dear Miss P.Q.,

I visited my Great Aunt Isabel recently in Iowa. My mother said I should send Aunt Isabel a little bread-and-butter note now that I am home. Mother left on a trip without telling me what a bread-and-butter note *is*. Does this mean I should send Aunt Isabel a bread-and-butter sandwich? Please explain.

Signed, Confused in Kansas

Miss P.Q.:   Oh, dear, you are confused! What a silly question! Don't you think the sandwich would get stale before it arrives? Think about it. Oops, sorry, I didn't mean to sound rude, but Miss P.Q. thought everyone knew what a bread-and-butter note was. Don't you children? [Waits for children to respond.] You don't know? Very well, it's a little thank you note for all the things Great Aunt Isabel did to make your visit pleasant. I have no idea why the note is called a bread-and-butter note. It just is. Do it! Aunt Isabel will be glad you wrote. Next question? Art, would you like to read one of the letters from my bag?

Art: Yes, Miss P. Q.

Dear Miss P.Q.,

My mother said I should never use my fingers when eating at a fancy restaurant. But here's the problem. Last night my friend's family took me to the Pomp-a-Door Palace, this really fancy place. The family told me to order anything I wanted. Well, I had heard all about lobsters so I ordered one. It sounded interesting and it was the most expensive thing on the menu! But you see, I had no idea a lobster was this ugly thing that came in a hard shell. My knife and fork didn't begin to cut through that. I just pretended I didn't feel like eating at all. What should I have done?

Signed, Hungry in Hartford, Connecticut

Miss P.Q.:   Thank you for reading that very sad letter, Art. This is what I wrote Hungry in Hartford.

Dear Hungry,

In the first place you should never, ever choose the most expensive thing on the menu. That is *VERY* bad manners, even though the family told you to order whatever you wanted. Next, you learned a hard lesson, didn't you? For goodness sake, don't order something you are so ignorant about. Lobsters are very tricky to eat. Didn't the waiter give you lobster crackers to crack the lobster? Lobster crackers look like something your Mom or Dad keeps in a toolbox. Next time, forget the lobster. Just order something easy like meatloaf. And don't pick it up in your fingers, either!

Signed, Miss P.Q.

Nancy: Miss P.Q., may I read the next question?

Miss P.Q.:   Certainly.

Nancy: Dear Miss P.Q.,

I want to have a birthday party for my eighth birthday. My dad said I cannot invite my friends Courtney and Kathy and Carrie and Cindy and Corey and Chris and all the other girls I know because that's too many kids. What should I do? I'm afraid somebody will get mad if she doesn't get an invitation and I will have no friends!

Signed, Worried in Washington.

Miss P.Q.: Well that one is really a hard question. Perhaps some of the children at our tea party today could answer Worried's question. [Ask for audience participation.] Thank you children. I will send some of your answers to this worried girl.

Art, do you have another question for me?

Art: I don't, but the person who wrote this letter does! I'll read the letter.

Dear Miss P.Q.,

We are going to my Uncle Sam's house for Thanksgiving dinner this year. Uncle Sam fixes green bean casserole every year. I absolutely hate green beans. How can I get out of eating them?

Signed, Sick in Santa Fe

Miss P.Q.: Dear Sick,

I have heard of children who don't like green beans. I have also heard of children doing all kinds of things not to eat food. My brother used to hide peas under his plate. Don't do that. You'll only get caught. My sister used to feed her carrots to our pet dog. It didn't work. The dog got sick. Well, I think you'd better try eating at least one green bean. It probably won't make you sick. Just hold your nose and stuff it in like this! [She demonstrates, using a fork.]

Art: Miss P.Q.?

Miss P.Q.: Yes, Art.

Art: I have a question of my own. May I ask it?

Miss P.Q.: Why yes, I believe we have time for one more. I hope it's a good one.

Art: Last week my mother was busy with the door closed to her home office, and she said it was nobody's business what she was doing and I shouldn't bother her.

Miss P.Q.: Yes, Art. What was the problem?

Art: Well, my teacher called on the phone to talk with my mother. And, of course, I knew I should tell the truth so—

Miss P.Q.: So what did you do, Art?

Art: So I told my teacher it was none of her business what my mother was doing and I hung up. Now Mom and my teacher are really mad at me. What did I do wrong?

Miss P.Q. (Fanning her face with a dinner napkin): Oh, Art! That was not smart! Did you really do that? Honesty is the best policy, but there is such a thing as being too honest. Perhaps somebody here in the room can help you? Does anyone have comments for Art? [Again, asks for audience participation.]

Thank you, children.

This is the end of Miss P.Q.'s letters for today. We hope you have had a lovely party. Please remember to thank the hostess at your table for serving you. And we hope you will come again to one of our library parties. Remember, mind your manners, and have a lovely day!

10

Friends Good and True

Today may be one of the most challenging times to teach friendship. We watch the television news, read daily newspaper accounts, and shake our heads over letters to the editor. We are assaulted by ads and movie previews. What can we think when we overhear children talking rudely to their parents. Dedicated elementary teachers say they need to retire early because children have become too unruly to teach. Probably every generation wonders what the world is coming to. But challenges of violence, abuse, anger, and intolerance around us cause me to read more, think longer, and try to write as cogently as I can about this important subject. These issues may seem beyond the scope of the chapter's topic, but they are the climate for addressing the subject of friendship.

In this light, we cannot be so naive as we have been. Times have changed dramatically from one generation to the next. Censoring unpleasant images and realistic books is not the answer. We all know that. Many kids spend hours playing violent video games, have already seen bloody images on television, and listen to song lyrics that encourage abusive responses. It seems a little late to tell victims of bullying to "just get over it" or to tell aggressive children to "just play fair" without stepping in. Librarians can introduce books on tough topics and hold honest discussions with kids. Teachers with the help of supportive administrators and smart counselors can guide kids through role-playing exercises. Educators can share stories of the consequences of poor choices. Displays and bulletin boards of good and bad behaviors can raise levels of consciousness. These are all areas that affect the abilities of children to make and keep friends.

This chapter and the previous one on manners work together, along with the chapter "Heart to Heart, Hand to Hand" in *Stories NeverEnding*. The books and activities provide positive ways to guide children through their lives. The bottom line that connects all of these subjects is the old Golden Rule to treat others as we would want to be treated. Positive examples of this adage can help children form good habits rather than resorting to preaching.

This chapter introduces a selection of books on friends and friendship. The programs for schools and public libraries differ. The school program "Let's Be Friends" includes activities for discussion and role-playing. It also introduces books on friends with related activities that children will do in cooperative pairs. Culminating projects for being good friends and citizens in the community, the nation, and our world will guide the librarian/teacher.

Children's librarians in public libraries can work hand-in-hand with schools. The program suggestions for schools can be a cooperative venture between schools and public libraries. The program "A Between Friends Party" for public libraries, however, extends the possibilities with a more light-hearted approach. Combining stories, food, crafts, and games, this party gives librarians and children a way to celebrate the joys of friendship with old and new friends.

Bibliography

Brown, Marc. *The True Francine*. Little Brown, 1981.

   Francine and Muffy are friends, but Muffy copies all of Francine's answers on a test. Since Muffy is the teacher's pet, Mr. Ratburn believes her when she says she did not cheat. Francine is punished, but in the end, Muffy confesses, and the friendship is renewed. Brown addresses the common problem of honesty and being true to your friend in this kid-appealing picture book. This author has written numerous stories about Arthur and his friends that are both popular and well written. *Arthur's Valentine* is especially appropriate for the topic of friendship.

Brown, Marc, and Laurie Krasny Brown. *How to Be a Friend: A Guide to Making Friends and Keeping Them*. Little, Brown, 1998.

   This cartoon format with speech balloons gives kids ideas about how to be a friend, learning to overcome shyness, techniques for dealing with bullies, handling arguments and making up.

Carlson, Nancy. *Sit Still*! Viking, 1996.

   Patrick has trouble sitting still and consequently seems to irritate most people around him. His wise mother helps him discover ways to keep physically active so he will feel better about himself. Although hyperactivity is not directly addressed in the book (and the family doctor is of little help to Patrick), parents and teachers of children with this disorder may find comfort in Patrick's story. Active children often need special help so they can make friends. Other good titles about friendship by this author include *I Like Me!* and *Arnie and the New Kid*.

Danzinger, Paula. *Forever Amber Brown*. Putnam's, 1996.

   In this Amber Brown book, the fourth grader is trying to accept her divorced mother's boyfriend and a best friend's move to Alabama. With great humor, Amber continues to enjoy her friendship with Brandi and gets to visit Justin in Alabama. All of the Amber Brown books entertain elementary school–age children, are light reading, and are not too difficult for children who have difficulty reading.

DeClements, Barthe. *The Pickle Song*. Viking, 1993.

   Paula is excited to have a new friend, Sukey, move into the neighborhood. Paula's family have struggled since her parents' divorce, but Paula learns that Sukey is living in a car with her mother. Paula's grandmother helps the homeless Sukey and her mother, and the girls become supportive friends. This story of friendship and struggle will be an eye-opener for some children and a great comfort to others.

Henkes, Kevin. *Jessica*. Greenwillow, 1989.

   Ruthie declares she has a friend named Jessica although her parents insist that the friend is imaginary. When Ruthie goes to school, she meets a little girl who offers to be a friend. Coincidentally, that little girl's name is Jessica. Imaginative children will love Henkes's understanding of this not-so-uncommon pattern of behavior. This author has written many excellent books dealing with friendship.

Hoberman, Mary Ann. *And to Think That We Thought That We'd Never Be Friends*. Illustrated by Kevin Hawkes. Dell Dragonfly, 1999.

   In this story in verse, a brother and sister get into fights but learn from their father that there are other ways to get along. This message spreads as the brother and sister extends their ideas and influence into the neighborhood and out into the world in one grand celebration of friendship.

Hurwitz, Joanna. *Oh No, Noah*! Seastar Books/North South, 2002.

Noah has moved to a new neighborhood and is nervous about making new friends. He isn't capable of doing tricks like some people, but he does have a strange object in his basement that fascinates the kids. Noah makes friends and learns about standing brave when others don't support you, and, in the end, the spunky girl next door stands up for him. This author has written dozens of good books about kids and friendship.

Lionni, Leo. *It's Mine!* Knopf, 1986.

Three selfish frogs quarrel over who owns the pond until they are threatened by a storm. They quickly see the value of sticking together and cooperating to survive. Lionni's story with a fable kind of wisdom will work for discussion about the nature of friendship and learning to get along.

Livingston, Irene. *Finklehopper Frog Cheers*. Illustrated by Brian Lies. Tricycle Press, 2005.

Ruby Rabbit helps Finklehopper Frog deflate bullies at the town picnic, and, in turn, Finklehopper insists that Ruby enter a race when she is afraid to compete against Kangaroo. This lively story will encourage kids to work together to face tough adversaries and bullies.

Lobel, Arnold. *Frog and Toad Are Friends*. Harper, 1970.

Five little stories about two good friends, the mirthful, well-meaning Frog, and the sometimes fretful but good-hearted Toad appeal to children from beginning readers to older kids who see the wisdom and humor in Lobel's Caldecott Honor Book. Other Lobel books about Frog and Toad include *Days with Frog and Toad* and *Frog and Toad Together.*

Ludwig, Trudy. *My Secret Bully*. Illustrated by Abigail Marble. River Wood Books, Tricycle Press, 2004.

This inspirational story about a girl whose best friend mistreats her and acts more like a bully instead of a caring friend gives all elementary school–age kids comfort and practical ways to handle this awkward situation. The outstanding story is a "must read," and the book also includes organizations, Web sites, and recommended readings on the subject for kids and for adults.

Marshall, James. *George and Martha Encore*. Houghton Mifflin, 1973.

Five little stories about two hippos that are good friends will interest young and older readers. The last story in this collection in which George plants fully bloomed tulips in Martha's garden to make her feel better about not being able to grow flowers ends with a perfect statement about friendship. "I would much rather have a friend like you than all the gardens in the world." Other titles about these friends include *George and Martha* and *George and Martha One Fine Day.*

Morrison, Lillian, compiler. *It Rained All Day That Night: Autograph Album Verses and Inscriptions.* August House, 2003.

Little verses, insults, endearments, and fun expressions kids have and continue to share with one another appear in a small, attractively designed book that kids will enjoy sharing or giving to one another. Such sections as "Yours till . . ." will inspire children to write their own expressions.

Nickell, Molli. *Guerrillas of Goodness Handbook*. Workman, 1994.

This little book of 127 ways to make a difference in the world by performing thoughtful acts of goodness will inspire children to think of even more ways to extend friendship into their communities at home or beyond their own backyard.

Palatini, Margie. *Stinky Smelly Feet: A Love Story*. Dutton, 2004.

Douglas and Dolores, two duck friends, enjoy going to the movies and to the beach, but Douglas's stinky feet seem to strain their friendship. Doris tries to help Douglas find solutions to his problem, but nothing seems to work. Fortunately their friendship survives anyway. This humorous picture book begs to be read aloud.

Paterson, Katherine. *Bridge to Terabithia*. Crowell, 1977.

This modern classic about the friendship between a fifth-grade girl and boy shows the importance of kids finding their own special places and addresses the difficulty in facing the death of a peer.

Ryder, Joanne. *Earthdance*. Illustrated by Norman Gorbty. Holt, 1996.

This lyrical text invites young readers to become connected to the earth and its wonders, and, in so doing, people will become connected to all of life. This book is not about friendship per se, but it reinforces the idea of making friends with everything and everyone on the earth.

Stauffacher, Sue. *Donuthead.* Knopf, 2003.

Franklin Delano Donuthead is a bright but very odd kid who is full of fear and has no friends his own age until the not-afraid-of-anything Sarah arrives at his school. Both children learn about overcoming obstacles and become friends. The overriding theme of treating others as you want to be treated makes this book a little treasure for teachers and librarians to read aloud in classrooms and libraries.

Vail, Rachel. *Sometimes I'm Bombaloo*. Illustrated by Yumi Heo. Scholastic, 2002.

This winning picture book about a little girl who learns to deal with anger and her explosive behavior will help many children work through barriers to friendship within their families and with friends. The graphic illustrations of emotions will inspire kids to draw their own pictures of the expression of feelings.

Wirths, Claudine G., and Mary Bowman-Kruhm. *Your Circle of Friends*. Twenty-First Century Books, Henry Holt, 1993.

Although this book appears in the Time to Be a Teen series, most of the questions are suitable for older elementary children. The format has kid appeal, and the content handles questions from keeping secrets to learning how to make hard choices when friendship may be in jeopardy.

Let's Be Friends: A Program for Schools

This is a great program for the school library media center, but it may also be planned for individual classrooms. Students from different grades can create the bulletin board or wall display or a small group of students can begin, with several classes continuing the effort. The books suggested for the "Let's Be Friends through Books" include many picture books. For older students, substitute longer titles from this chapter's bibliography. I like to use some picture books with upper elementary students if the ideas in the books can open discussion on different levels. The projects described for the final activity can be planned for one class or grade or become long-term projects involving students from the entire school.

Materials Needed

No special materials needed for these projects

Procedure

1. Plan a "Good Friends Picture Board" ahead of time by cutting out magazine photographs, locating pictures on the Internet, or assigning children to bring in pictures of their own. See the picture board suggestion sheet in this chapter to help you get started. Have students place these on the bulletin board or display wall. Add questions and mottos if you like. For example, "Why is she angry?" "Fighting to Fight? Fighting to Win?" You may decide to just place pictures on the board with no "prompts" then lead a class discussion the next day.

2. After engaging in a spirited discussion based on the picture board, distribute speech balloons and thought balloons with questions and comments based on suggestions in the "Bad News–Good News" section in this chapter. In small groups, students work cooperatively to write both poor and better responses to communications. For example, the loaded question, "What's *your* problem?" speech balloon, might have some of these response speech balloons: "Would you rephrase that question, please?" (spoken politely); "Are you asking me?"; "It sounds like you are upset. Are you?" Note that there are no right or wrong responses, simply responses that may escalate or deescalate the emotion in the original speech balloon.

3. In a third class session, the librarian/teacher introduces the topic "Let's Be Friends through Books" by reading aloud one or two of the books listed in the section of this name. For each book read, students will answer a question or do an activity. Divide the class into pairs to choose a book from the "Friends through Books" list. Each pair will then read the book together and do the activity to share with the class as a whole.

4. Students share their "Let's Be Friends through Books" activities.

5. The librarian/teacher reads *Earthdance* and introduces community and global projects about friendship to be completed at a future date.

Good Friends Picture Board

Find pictures and photographs of people exhibiting these feelings or in these situations to make a display board collage. This is simply a starter list.

1. A person showing anger through a facial expression

2. A person acting out anger (throwing a tantrum or throwing things)

3. Two people fighting

4. Children playing a combative kind of game such as tug-of-war

5. Someone putting another person down such as one person shaking a finger at another

6. An embarrassed person

7. A person with a disability struggling to do something

8. One person helping another

9. Two people in a caring situation

10. A group of kids with diversity (ethnic, different ages, different sizes)

11. A shy person

12. An angry crowd

13. A happy crowd

14. Two people excluding another person

15. People engaged in a group activity

Bad News–Good News

Draw speech balloons (the kind you see in newspaper cartoons) and write expressions within the speech balloons that might cause hurt, defensiveness, or another block to good communications. Distribute these to students and instruct them to write responses that might defuse the negative comment.

The following list of expressions could include:

1. "What's *your* problem?"

2. "You're no fun!"

3. "What a lousy idea."

4. "You like *that* book????"

5. "My sister says you cheated on the test."

6. "Where did you get *that* jacket?"

7. "You're a liar!"

8. "I'm smarter than you are!"

9. "You talk funny."

10. "It's your fault!"

Draw thought balloons (the kind you see in newspaper comic pages) and write expressions within the thought balloons. Instruct students to think of situations that might have prompted the thought. The idea here is to show kids that sometimes we make wrong assumptions and think of things that were not intended at all.

1. Maybe I'm not very attractive after all.

2. I didn't know I sounded angry.

3. She makes me feel dumb.

4. Those kids are so snobby.

5. I didn't do it.

6. What's wrong with me?

7. Uh-oh, I'm going to be in trouble now!

8. I'll never fit in.

9. Do I look that awful?

10. I can't show it, but I'm scared.

Let's Be Friends through Books

The library media specialist reads one or two books about friends or social behaviors aloud then proceeds with the activity suggested. Then, student teams select another book to read and do the suggested activity from the list provided. Add other books of your own to this list.

Book to Read Aloud: *Stinky Smelly Feet: A Love Story* by Margie Palatini

Book Annotation Activity: Douglas and Doris, two wacky ducks, are smitten with each other, but Douglas's stinky feet turn off Doris repeatedly. Rather than read the entire book at first, read only a few pages, ending at the line, "He, of course, was very embarrassed about having stinky, smelly feet." Stop and ask students to identify the problem and suggest three solutions. In addition, brainstorm with students what Dolores might have said instead of blurting out "Put on your shoes! ... You have stinky, smelly feet!"

Finish reading the book and ask two students to role play the parts of Douglas and Doris. Younger students might use puppets to reenact the story.

Book to Read Aloud: *Sometimes I'm Bombaloo* by Rachel Vail

Book Annotation and Activity: Kate, a "really good kid," sometimes loses her temper and acts this out with her fists and by yelling. She learns about cooling off but, at the time, is too angry to do it. Do a guided imagery exercise by having students think about a situation that makes them very angry. Then ask them to show the anger with their faces and with body language. Finally, ask students to try different physical movements to expel anger such as stretching tall, hitting an imaginary punching bag, and then hanging arms limply at sides. Have students draw or paint pictures of angry faces inspired by the evocative illustrations in this book. The angry face pictures may be done on paper plates to use later as facemasks. A happy, relaxed face may then be drawn on the opposite side of the plate.

Friends through Books List

A brief phrase or annotation describes the situation in each book with a brief activity described. Flesh out these skeleton ideas as you like. Check the bibliography of this chapter for complete bibliographic citations.

1. *Sit Still!* by Nancy Carlson.

    Hyperactivity

    Creative dramatics, brainstorm solutions

2. *And to Think That We Thought That We'd Never Be Friends* by Mary Ann Hoberman

    Various potentially troublesome situations followed by a solution

    Creative dramatics, draw comic strips

3. "The Letter" from *Frog and Toad Are Friends* by Arnold Lobel

    Toad is sad because no one ever writes him a letter but Frog surprises him.

    Make cheer-up cards or write letters to Toad

4. *It's Mine* by Leo Lionni

    Quarrelsome frogs learn to share when faced with danger

List situations in which sharing is difficult for class discussion

Draw pictures or find photos of people sharing

5. "Wayne" and "Joshua" from *Sad Underwear* by Judith Viorst

Two poems about kids, one is a "loser" and the other is "too good to be true"

Act out or read aloud to class, draw cartoon strips

6. *Rotten Island* by William Steig

Bad behavior changes when beauty arrives

Comic strip retelling, rotten art projects, creative dramatics

7. *Keeping Up with Roo* by Sharlee Glenn

Friendship with mentally disabled relative

Journal writing, writing poems, role-playing

8. *Just Enough and Not Too Much* by Kaethe Zemach

Too many things doesn't leave room or time for friends

Creative dramatics, collages of things, displays

9. *Rose and Dorothy* by Roslyn Schwartz

Friends who are very different from each other fight, and then make up

Journal writing, puppet plays

10. *Roses Are Pink and Your Feet Really Stink* by Diane deGroat

Nasty valentines cause friendship problems

Making valentines, poetry writing

Community and Global Friends Project List

Use this list as you brainstorm ideas with your students about one or more projects the class can do for your community, state, the country, or an international organization or cause.

1. Pick up trash along a roadway or in a park.

2. Offer class services to a grocery or department store in which kids can help people with disabilities or elderly with finding items on a grocery list or carrying items.

3. Raise money to provide gloves and mittens for a community agency distributing clothing to the needy.

4. Read books aloud to people in a hospital or nursing home.

5. Collect canned goods and necessary paper products for a community food bank, especially during the winter (not just at holiday time).

6. Begin a "give a little, save a little" from your allowance program. Make class banks to collect money in these two categories. The money collected can be given to a local charity.

7. Do research on the Internet to find international organizations dedicated to conservation and a cleaner environment.

8. Collect toys in good condition to take to a needy day-care program.

9. Collect children's books in good condition to send to an after-school program for kids at risk.

10. "Adopt" a local community organization and find out what service or equipment they need to have funded then raise money to help.

A Between Friends Party: Program for Public Libraries

This crafts, food, stories, and games program sets the stage for kids to share fun projects with their friends, old and new. It could be planned for an hour or as an open-house drop-in event. The steps listed in the procedures section could be used either as sequence of events or as different activity centers that go on simultaneously.

Materials Needed

1. Platter for poem cards

2. Macramé cording, embroidery thread, or twine for friendship bracelets

3. Notepaper for friendship notes

4. Colored card stock for friendship bookmarks

5. Assorted stickers and rubber stamps for making bookmarks

6. Ingredients for friendship sandwiches (check recipes in this chapter to make your own list)

Procedure

1. Read aloud *Stinky Smelly Feet,* prompting kids to repeat the phrase "Peeee Yew" at appropriate places in the story.

2. Reenact several stories from the Frog and Toad books as readers' theatre or with puppets.

3. Collect friendship poems such as Shel Silverstein's "Hug o' War," "Helping," "Don't Tell Me," and "Won't You?" Write each poem out on a big index card and stack them on a platter or plate. The leader reads the first poem, "Just Between Friends: Take One and Pass It On" (provided later) then passes the platter to another person to read the second poem then passes it on. Note that the "Just Between Friends" poem is short and catchy. You may want to have kids clap it out or do it as a call and response chant. Fill the platter with enough poems to let everyone in the group read a different poem.

4. Make friendship crafts projects such as friendship bookmarks, friendship notepaper, or friendship bracelets. Two Internet sites with instructions for making friendship bracelets are the following:

    http://tax.shopnetmall.com/www.funroom.com/summer/macrame.html

    http://www.makingfriends.com/macrame.htm

Supply children with a box full of stickers and hand stamps to decorate notepaper (cut 8 1/2 x 11–inch paper to half size for notepaper). Cut strips of brightly colored card stock approximately 2 x 7 inches for bookmarks.

5. Play cooperative games. You can adapt old-fashioned competitive games to transform them into cooperation-everyone-wins games. For example, play musical chairs in reverse. Begin with children walking around a circle with one chair placed in the middle. Play music, and when it stops, one child sits down. A second chair is added and play resumes. To increase the musical chair chain faster, add chairs two at a time until everyone is seated.

Tell children they are making a friendship machine. One person is designated the "engine" and does an action. This child chooses another child to add a part to the machine. This child might be the "wing" with one hand touching the shoulder of the "engine" and her other arm flapping. Another child adds another part to the machine and so on until every child is attached in friendship.

6. Make and eat friendship sandwiches following the recipe suggestions on page 183 or share international foods in a spirit of world friendship.

Just Between Friends: Take One and Pass It On

Sharing Stories
Jokes so silly
Aren't you just
A silly dilly!
Cross your heart
Don't know why
You're my favorite
Kind of guy!
Make a wish
Turn and twirl
You're my favorite
Kind of girl!
Friendship rings
And valentines
Tell me, friend,
Won't you be mine?
Through ups and downs
Through thick and thin

Good friends let you
Sometimes win.
Cheer me on
When I'm trying
Understand
When I'm crying.
Let's make friends
Old and new
I like me
And I like you!
Read a poem
Let it rhyme
Be my friend
Anytime!
Take a poem
Pass it on
Going, going

Sandwich Platter Suggestions

Danish open-faced sandwiches inspired these suggestions. A volunteer could make several platters of these sandwiches for children to enjoy, or you could assemble ingredients with little "recipes" for each sandwich and invite children to make their own.

Authentic Danish sandwiches (*smorrebrod*) would include some rather exotic ingredients that many American children might not like, and they are expensive for a crowd. Those of us who love herring, anchovies, liver paste, salmon, and shrimp know that children will probably prefer eggs, chicken, cheese, and fruit.

Begin with thin slices of firm bread, especially wheat, pumpernickel, and rye bread. Spread a small slice of bread with butter and add other ingredients. Try small squares, circles, triangles, or diamond shapes for a nice, decorative touch. Here are some combinations that children like.

1. Cheese and apple sandwiches: Place a slice of cheddar cheese on the buttered bread and add a thin slice of apple.

2. Cheese and orange sandwich: Spread cream cheese on bread and add an orange slice (remove rind).

3. Chicken spread sandwich: Combine 1 cup chopped cooked chicken, 2 to 3 tablespoons mayonnaise, and 1 tablespoon sweet pickle relish or crushed pineapple.

4. Chive butter sandwich: Cream 1/2 cup softened butter with 2 tablespoons chopped chives and add a 1/2 teaspoon Worcestershire sauce. Spread on dark bread.

5. Fruit butter sandwich: Cream together 1/2 cup soft butter and 2 tablespoons chopped craisins or cranberries with 1 tablespoon grated orange peel. Spread on white or wheat bread.

6. Egg salad sandwich: Combine 4 chopped hard-cooked eggs with 1 teaspoon minced onion, 1/2 teaspoon mustard, 1 tablespoon pickle relish, and 1/2 cup mayonnaise. Spread on rye or pumpernickel bread.

7. Ham, cheese, and apple sandwich: Chop or grind 1 cup ham and spread on buttered bread. Add a thin slice of Swiss or cheddar cheese and a thin slice of apple.

8. Cucumber sandwich: Spread firm white bread with butter and add a thin slice of cucumber.

Appendix

Planning an Author Visit

This checklist will help school media specialists and public librarians plan actual author visits. In many communities, schools and public libraries work jointly to bring authors to an area. Joint committees of representatives raise money and plan publicity and events. Lawrence, Kansas, for example, planned a "community read" event in November 1999 during which Avi's book *Nothing but the Truth* was read throughout the town. The school district and public library jointly sponsored a visit from the author and planned various events held in schools, the library, and different places at the University of Kansas.

I. Choosing the Right Author

    A. Consider the age level with whom the author will work.

    B. Decide what the visit should accomplish (set criteria). Example: Do you want the author to interact with the students in specific ways or on specific topics?

    C. Begin an investigation for an author.

        1. Talk with media specialists, librarians, bookstore owners, and writers' groups.

        2. Attend authors' presentations at educational, library, and literature conferences, as well as bookstore-sponsored events.

        3. Contact publishers and ask for recommendations of authors who meet the criteria you have established and who are within your budget.

II. Advance Planning for Visit

    A. Contact the publisher to invite the author and establish the fee. Also consult authors' Web sites. Some writers provide information about their fees and schedules on sites.

    B. Determine how the visit will be financed. Possible sources include:

        1. Parent organizations

        2. Professional organizations

        3. Community organizations

        4. Joint sponsorship with schools, libraries, and businesses

        5. Sale of author's books

        6. Fundraising activities such as book fairs, carnivals, and so on

    C. Verify the commitment with the author in writing.

        1. Define parameters—scheduling, format of sessions, group size.

        2. Clearly define date, time, transportation arrangements, and fees.

        3. Determine whether author is interested in additional engagements while in the area.

        4. If autographing sessions are planned, establish procedures, times, author's preferences, and so on.

D. If books are sold and autographed, consult with publishers about discounts, policies on returns, postages, and so on.

E. Make arrangements for lodging and meals. Establish procedures for payment with the hotel prior to the visit.

F. Arrange for transportation during the author's stay.

G. Plan publicity

1. Newspapers, newsletters, Web site announcements

2. Promotional materials such as posters, brochures, and even campaign-style buttons (Lawrence, Kansas, passed out clever buttons with the message "Have You Read It?" to promote the Avi community read events.)

3. Television and radio announcements

III. Curriculum and Library Planning Pre-Activities

A. Read aloud at least one book by the author in school libraries and classrooms to develop a common basis for discussion. Read a chapter of a book and booktalk other books in public libraries.

B. Promote reading other books by the author in small groups or in public library book clubs.

C. Use art projects, creative dramatics exercises, readers' theatre, and other activities to further promote interest in the author's works.

IV. Day of the Visit

A. Provide a warm, inviting atmosphere for students, staff, and the author.

B. Display student artwork promoting the author's work.

C. Plan carefully down to the last minute, remembering to include breaks. Then be flexible enough to deal with the unexpected. Be certain to have plenty of volunteers available to help.

D. Set up autographing tables, slips for students to write their names for author's ease in personalizing the inscriptions, and volunteers to help the author keep the session moving along efficiently.

E. Plan special meal events but also consult with the author's wishes. Some authors appreciate a little break in the day on their own or with a smaller group.

F. Consider videotaping the event, but be certain to get the author's permission well in advance of the day.

V. Post-Activities

A. In schools, have small group discussions about the students' ideas and impressions.

B. Read further books by the author.

C. Hold a meeting with the planning committee to evaluate the event and read any evaluation forms teachers or librarians have completed to make recommendations for future events of this kind.

D. Give students opportunities to engage in their own writing/publishing projects, and discuss the authoring process. Schools are accustomed to this kind of follow-up, and public libraries may wish to have writing contests or begin student writing clubs after a successful author visit.

Note: *This document is a revision of the original that appeared in* Fanfares: Programs for Classrooms and Libraries *(Libraries Unlimited, 1990). It was first written by Ann Holton, Mick Moore, and Martha Melton of the Iowa City Community School District. I have revised their work based on my own experiences as an author and a librarian and also updated the document to reflect greater use of technology in libraries and schools.*

Favorite Fantasy Titles from Librarians

In a questionnaire regarding fantasy literature, librarians expressed that children at their facilities found fantasy appealing because it gave them an opportunity to use their imagination. Kids like stories that could "never really happen," and they could put themselves in the place of the hero of such stories. Some librarians suggested that fantasy was a kind of escapism that is perhaps needed in our difficult times.

Most librarians mentioned the Harry Potter books as especially significant. One librarian felt that Rowling "blasted open the door and once kids found delight in the world of fantasy and escape from the world, they couldn't get enough." In addition to Rowlings books, the following titles were listed:

1. Alexander, Lloyd. The Chronicles of Prydian (series). Holt.

2. Avi. *Poppy.* Orchard, 1995.

3. Babbitt, Natalie. *Tuck Everlasting.* Farrar, 1975.

4. Cleary, Beverly. *The Mouse and the Motorcycle.* Morrow, 1965.

5. Collins, Suzanne. *Gregor the Overlander.* Scholastic, 2000.

6. Cooper, Susan. The Dark Is Rising (series). Margaret McElderry.

7. Coville, Bruce. *Into the Land of the Unicorns.* Scholastic, 1994.

8. Dicamillo, Kate. *The Tale of Despereaux.* Candlewick, 2003.

9. Eager, Edward. *Half Magic.* Harcourt Brace, 1954.

10. Funke, Cornelia Caroline. *Inkheart.* Translated from the German by Anthea Bell. Scholastic, Chicken House, 2003.

11. Gannett, Ruth S. *My Father's Dragon.* Random House, 1948.

12. Hoeye, Michael. *Time Stops for No Mouse.* Terfle Books, 2000.

13. Jacques, Brian. *Loamhedge.* Philomel, 2003.

14. Jones, Diana Wynne. *A Tale of Time City.* Greenwillow, 1987.

15. Juster, Norton. *The Phantom Tollbooth.* Random House, 1989.

16. L'Engle, Madeleine. *A Wrinkle in Time.* Yearling, 1962.

18. Lewis, C. S. The Chronicles of Narnia (series). Harper.

19. Lowry, Lois. *The Giver.* Houghton Mifflin, 1993.

20. McGraw, Eloise. *The Moorchild.* Margaret K. McElderry Books, 1996.

21. Norton, Mary. *The Borrowers.* Harcourt, 1953.

22. O'Brien, Robert C. *Mrs. Frisby and the Rats of NIMH.* Atheneum, 1971.

23. Pearce, Philippa. *Tom's Midnight Garden.* J. B. Lippincott, 1958.

24.   Pierce, Tamora. *Alanna: The First Adventure.* Atheneum, 1983.

25.   Pullman, Philip. *The Golden Compass.* Knopf (distributed by Random House), 1995.

26.   Rodda, Emily. Rowan of Rin (series). Greenwillow.

27.   Rubinstein, Gillian. *Space Demons.* Puffin, 1988.

28.   Sendak, Maurice. *Where the Wild Things Are.* Harper, 1963.

29.   Snicket, Lemony. A Series of Unfortunate Events (series). Harper.

30.   Tolkein, J. R. R. *The Hobbit.* Houghton Mifflin, 1937.

31.   Waugh, Sylvia. *The Mennyms.* Morrow, 1994.

32.   White, E. B. *Charlotte's Web.* Harper, 1952.

33.   Winthrop, Elizabeth. *The Castle in the Attic.* Holiday House, 1985.

34.   Wrede, Patricia. *Dealing with Dragons.* Harcourt Brace Jovanovich, 1990.

Note: Many thanks to the following librarians for their fantasy book suggestions: Carol Elbert, Ames, Iowa; Joyce Steiner, Lawrence Public Library, Lawence, KS; Children's librarians from the Kansas City Missouri Public Library Systems and the Johnson County Kansas Library System.

Index

About the Author

JAN IRVING is a full time writer and consultant in the field of children's literature and library services to children. She has been a librarian and children's library supervisor in Iowa, Kansas, and Colorado; conducted workshops and presented public addresses nationally; has been active in the American Library Association for twenty five years and is now a member of the Writers Place, an organization for readers and writers in Kansas City, Missouri. In addition to her professional books, Jan writes poetry, children's books, and is exploring new genres for her writing and artistic skills. She lives in Overland Park, Kansas, with her husband Bill, who is also retired from the library profession.